BlackSide Of The White House

A MEMOIR FOR GENERATIONS TO COME

Pierpont Morgan Mobley

Curry Brothers Publishing

ISBN: 979-8-9907516-2-0 Softbound
ISBN: 979-8-9907516-3-7 Hardbound

Request for information should be addressed to: Curry Brothers Marketing and Publishing Group

P.O. Box 247 Haymarket, VA 20168

Cover Design: Vibranium Media Group
Executive Editing: Tiffany Johnson

CURRY BROS.
MARKETING + PUBLISHING GROUP

BlackSide Of The White House

A MEMOIR FOR GENERATIONS TO COME

Pierpont Morgan Mobley

Curry Brothers Publishing

Dedication

To Jeannette my dear wife, partner and friend of more than 50 years who has been my Rock for her continued support throughout these many years of complete joy and happiness.

I also express a special appreciation for our son Tony and our daughter Patricia for being on this journey with me and who studied alongside me when I was in law school. Patricia has followed me professionally in Human Resources helping others while Tony, a professional photographer, specializes in social justice.

Amazing Gratefulness

And to Vickie my daughter-in-law, Deja, and Jada granddaughters, and our many friends that, kept encouraging me to write this book and motivated me to continue to lend my EEO, Human Rights and Civil Rights to all!

In addition, to my older brother, M. Clarence Mobley and his wife Grace of more than 50 years and the other Mobley's and the Dunbar family and Alonzo (Al) and Elnora Marshall.

Thank you to Denise Wright, PhD, Editor, who was instrumental in helping me with the initial writing of the book and Windy Carson Smith for her final review.

My ongoing inspiration has been from my church of more than 45 years, The Second New Saint Paul Baptist Church, in Washington, DC who has always supported me and my entire family and the Armstrong Tech H.S. Alumni Association for their support.

And

Deacon Rick Lee, "The Praying Man" and his family and Magruder and Andrea Murray and the current and former Hausas Club Members and their families.

In Memory of

To Dr(s). Janette & Rudy Harris, who transitioned in 2020, provided inspiration for writing this memoir.

Pierpont's Influence

(Co-workers, Family & Friends)

S TATEMENT of Viola Harkins McIver

RE: Mr. Pierpont Mobley

I had the opportunity to work in Jimmy Carter's campaign in Georgia. After his successful election, I received a call from Hamilton Jordan, President Carter's Chief of Staff, who allowed me to have my historic moment by assigning me as the first female *Usher* to work in the West Wing.

I was later reassigned to the correspondence unit where I received and answered mail sent to the President. I was the only African American in that office and from day one I knew my coworkers were not happy when I walked into the room.

The second day I was there I met Pierpont Mobley, and I was so happy when he walked into the room to greet me. I truly believe God knew I needed this man in my life as I was only 25 years old and needed help navigating the culture. He was always there to help me and others who needed guidance.

One such help came when I was turned down for a loan at the White House Credit Union with no explanation unlike my coworkers who were getting loans to buy cars and homes.

I happened to mention to Pierpont that I was denied a loan and felt it was because I was black. The only thing he said was "oh" and said to apply again.

After getting word that my loan was approved, I asked what happened and he simply said they made a mistake.

I am so happy that he is telling his story!

Viola Harkins McIver

~~~~~~

Family Statement

Wife, Daughter, Son, Daughter-in-law and granddaughters

To see Pierpont finally achieve his lifelong dream of publishing his book is truly a blessing.

He experienced discrimination and racial profiling as a young black man he was so determined to get his law degree so he could help others with Equal Employment Opportunity issues. It took him 16 years to get through all his education while working full time jobs and serving in the D.C. National Guard. There were times when I marveled at how he studied alongside our children.

I do believe that he can lay claim that he is the only Black to serve in the White House Personnel office under four different administrations. But believe me it was not without sacrifice as we know he encountered rough times while there, but he hung in because he put his family first.

He has always been the "wind" beneath not only my wings but our family's. We thank God for his unselfish love, his perseverance, love of family and community!

Patricia, Tony, Vickie and granddaughters Deja and Jada are proud of you for leaving a written legacy and how you allowed your knowledge and experience over the years to be a blessing to so many others.

Lovingly,
Your family,
Jeannette, Patricia, Tony & Victoria, Deja and Jada

~~~~~~

"When I ran for Council in 2012, I was fortunate to have the support of Pierpont Mobley and his wife, Jeannette, during my campaign. His knowledge of the District of Columbia and its intersection in our federal and local political structure made him an indispensable advisor to me. Pierpont shared his guidance and wisdom with our entire team, and I have been fortunate to call upon him time and again to receive critical input that is informed by sage experience.

For far too long in our city's history, many of our federal edifices and agencies shut out people like Pierpont Mobley. Thankfully, his talents and tenaciousness led him to serve four successive presidents at The White House and he became the first African American to be appointed in a professional position in the White House Personnel Office. His 32 years of federal service spanned several agencies where his expertise in civil rights, human rights, and equal employment opportunity drew awareness and action to individuals and communities in need of fairness across our country.

Pierpont's commitment to our great city continues today through the service and activism he and his wife still deliver to our community. His groundbreaking story serves as a shining example to us all.

Kenyan R. McDuffie
Council member At Large
Chair Pro Tempore
Council of the District of Columbia

~~~~~~

"As one of our Nation's top equal opportunity advocate, activist and history trailblazer, Pierpont Mobley's tremendous career has focused on expanding employment opportunities in various Federal Government Agencies, during four U.S. Presidential Administrations. Pierpont's internal fortitude and brilliant intellect is evident throughout his book. His powerful personal story, as transposed over his professional career achievements shines a light on his wonderful life of self-sacrifice, commitment, and dedication to our Nation. Congratulations and thank you, Pierpont for this MUST-READ book that will be an inspiration to all generations."

Attorney Kerwin E. Miller, USNA Class of 1975

~~~~~~

Congratulations to Pierpont!

I am pleased to write a few words of support for a good friend, civic leader, and family man, Pierpont Mobley. I have known and worked with Pierpont at various levels of service in the District of Columbia. Like *Nehemiah* in the Bible, Pierpont prepared himself for service by finishing college and Antioch Law School so he could spend a life of service advocating for individuals who found themselves discriminated against in the workplace and in the community. He has volunteered his unique knowledge, motivational and character-building skills at Ballou High School, Henley Elementary and Luke C Moore Academy High over the years and mentored many young men and women in the federal government and the community.

Although Pierpont is a very modest man who seeks no honor and recognition for his lifelong work, he has been honored with Resolutions from Washington D.C. City Council, recognition from Presidents Carter, Nixon, Obama, and most recently received President Biden's Lifetime Achievement Award for his volunteerism.

As the Founding Director of the African American Civil War Memorial and Museum in Washington, I have relied on the wise counsel and insights from Pierpont and his wife Jeannette, to help me along the way. I am proud to offer these few words of encouragement and for Pierpont, a shining example of dedicated service and civic engagement. I can't wait to read his book.

Frank Smith, PhD.
Founding Director, African American Civil War Museum

~~~~~~

"Pioneer" is a term that one hears a lot in middle and senior high schools. "First" is a word that usually comes to mind when defining a pioneer; Lewis and Clark, for example, first scramble through the bushes and the brambles to create path to the Oregon Territory. Neil Armstrong and "Buzz" Aldrin first blazed a path to the moon. I want to speak to another genre of pioneer who has made his mark much closer to the Washington DC area.

Pierpont Mobley is a unique and much unheralded person who has successfully blazed many trails in assessing others to navigate the ebbs and flow of human relationships. Whether by mediation or by arbitration, Mr. Mobley 's thirty years in EEO and HR management has calmed the swells of discord in countless human interactions. His record of achievement earned him a lifetime Achievement Award from President Biden, an accomplishment that few can claim.

I learned of his work at a social club – The Hausas – when we both were members. Social Club or not, Mr. Mobley would often take a meeting floor to rail about the injustices that he had witnessed in his work and of his efforts to address them. Even there he would stand arms and hips akimbo giving full measure of his rage that were associated with to the EEO/HR issues that had come before him at work.

As has been with the known cases of Lewis and Clark and Armstrong, Mr. Mobley's knowledge and contributions to the zeitgeist of history have brought light and justice to the society that he has help form, Lewis, Clark and Armstrong earned their status as historical pioneers. Pierpont Mobley is, and has earned his as well as continuing to fight for what he and others think is right. He has truly been a pioneer in his own right.

The Hausas Club

~~~~~~

CONGRESSWOMAN ELEANOR HOLMES NORTON
1300 PENNSYLVANIA AVENUE N.W., SUITE M-1000
WASHINGTON, DC 20004-3002
VOICE: 202-408-9041   FAX: 202-408-9048

~~~~~~

Pierpont and his wife Jeannette are 2 of my dearest friends who became supporters of my run for Congress since my first election in 1990.

Our relationship spans several decades. I was appointed the first woman Chair of the Equal Employment Opportunity Commission by President Jimmy Carter while Pierpont was appointed as the first African American professional in the White House Personnel Office.

When I need any help or support, I know that I can call Pierpont. Since my first term in Congress, Pierpont has selflessly served on my Congressional Service Academy Selection Committee, which nominates students to the U.S. military schools. He has also carved out time to be part of my Congressional Black Caucus Scholarship Committee for several years. All of this in addition to helping make sure I am elected every 2 years.

Pierpont's charisma, charm, and all-around jovial spirit, along with his love for his wife, are his signature. He is a light in every room and a proverbial Knight in Shining Armor.

Pierpont Morgan Mobley: A Black Man of Good Will:

For more than 10 years, Pierpont has been one of our "Council of Elders" for the 100 Fathers, Inc. Our organization is one that focuses on empowering our black youths within the DMV.

We pride ourselves on being proactive involved in assisting families in all aspects of fatherhood development that is often missing in our family structures.

As one of our volunteers, Mr. Mobley plays a major role in counseling and mentoring our youths when we conduct training workshops. He is effective at coaching young men to accept responsibility as a parent and understanding the importance of being self-sufficient and taking control of their lives. As a result, he is highly respected in these sessions. He has the capacity to display empathy to their situations yet can have stern conversations when needed.

Prior to Mobley becoming a member of 100 Fathers, Inc., we were aware of his dedication in the realm of civil and human rights. As a way of inspiring our young men, we often call upon him to share his inspiring story of how he went from a high school laggard who spent his days in pool halls to turning his life around to what it is today.

We congratulate Pierpont on the launch of his book because it is a story needs telling.

Dr. Franklyn Malone, PhD, CEO Founder, The 100 Father's inc.
Ordinary Men Doing extraordinary things

This is on behalf of Pierpont Mobley service's at USDA.

As a former Program Analyst for USDA, and a retired Major in the Army Reserves, I filed a discrimination complaint against my agency because of my race, black, when I was not selected for a GM-14 position that I was over qualified for and a white female was selected for the position, in questioned. She had very little experience for this position. I had been in a similar position and felt that I was much more qualified than she was. Most of my co-workers were very upset that she was selected over me. I had served in this Division for more than six years. I found out that she had friends in the Director's office. Therefore, I filed my complaint to the Office of EEO and HR. Pierpont, who was the EEO Complaints Manager, assisted me in my case. Mr. Mobley resolved my dispute in two months, and I received my promotion. He was very well respected at the agency. He was well versed and qualified in EEO law. He often resolved similar cases throughout the agency of 122,000 employees.

R. Johnson

~~~~~~

Second New St. Paul Baptist Church

First giving honor to our Lord and Savior, Jesus Christ.

On behalf of Pastor Nathaniel Benjamin, Jr., the officers, and members of Second New St. Paul Baptist Church, we extend our love and congratulations to Bro. Pierpont Mobley, for the release of his book, The Black Side of the White House.

Bro. Mobley has been a member of our church for more than 40 years. During his Christian Walk he has served in a variety of ministry positions; Youth Fellowship Ministry, Chairperson, Brotherhood Ministry, Men's Day Drive, Chairperson and most importantly; a resolute member who supports his church. With his wife and children watching, he was honored as "Father of the Year."

Our members know of his background in civil and human rights and often call upon him for advice which he readily gives. Our late Pastor, Rev. Dr. Edgar L. Williams, Sr. observed his many attributes and with the support of the officers of the church; selected him to train as a Deacon. Bro. Mobley was truly honored, but his heart was with the youth of our church. As a man of God, Pastor Williams continued to keep him as a close confidant.

To our surprise and as a testament to him and the work of our church; Bro. Mobley recommended Pastor Williams' induction into the D.C. Hall of Fame. He had a great love and respect for his Pastor who led his family spiritually and kept them in prayer.

We are incredibly grateful for his service to humanity and for the Lord sending him to this branch of Zion. We are especially proud of his service in the Personnel Office at the White House under four Presidents and we thank him for his continued support of the church and its ministries. We wish him all the best with his book. To God Be the Glory!

Because of Calvary, we are the officers and members of Second New St. Paul Baptist Church:

Rev. Nathaniel Benjamin, Jr., Pastor

~~~~~~

As a young rising professional in the field of affirmative action, equal employment opportunity, inclusion, and diversity, I had the privilege of being mentored by the imitable Mr. Pierpont Morgan Mobley—a trailblazer and leader in the profession. As some may believe themselves to be called to this arduous profession and assignment, in actuality few are chosen. Mr. Mobley was chosen for this unenviable undertaking.

Maturity has allowed me to earnestly understand and appreciate him as a polemarch, exemplar, and model of excellence. In the seasons of rapidly changing and schizophrenic civil rights legislation, Mr. Mobley has been an unswerving constant. He is a steadfast soldier for social justice; an ardent advocate for the disenfranchised, marginalized, minoritized, otherized, and discriminated; and a vociferous ally to those rendered mute because of the pain and stain resulting from micro-aggressive and oppressive behavior. He is a truth teller and generous griot—the authentic archivist and narrator of his lived experiences, as well as others.

With uncompromised integrity and contagious positive energy, Mr. Mobley is courageous, humble, respected, and principled. So many stand on his shoulders, including me. It is an honor to call him my elder, friend, and mentor.

Dr. Michelle T. Scott
Special Assistant to the President for Board Relations, Operations, and Services Office of the President
Montgomery College

~~~~~~

I am writing to express my sincere gratitude for the empathetic, passionate, and outstanding legal representation provided by Mr. Pierpont Mobley, when I was on the "receiving end" of a "wrongful termination" action. To describe my case as onerous would be an understatement. However, despite such obstacles, Mr. Mobley remained undaunted. In fact, his passionate legal representation was awe-inspiring. He ferreted through the voluminous record quickly and created a winning strategy. As a result of his endeavors, the case went to mediation and was settled quickly for an amount in excess of what I expected.

In addition to his excellent legal acumen, Mr. Mobley possesses great empathy. Litigation is a difficult process which can leave parties emotionally and psychologically drained. I was no exception. Fortunately, Mr. Mobley's compassionate "ear" provided me with the support that I needed to keep fighting. He believed in me and that made all the difference. Mr. Mobley listens, cares, and possesses superb legal skills. He wins, and I am sincerely thankful to have had his representation.

T. Clark

~~~~~~

"As a very young professional (having just graduated from HBCU Spelman College in Atlanta, GA), moving to the Nation's Capital with President Jimmy Carter, I never would have survived at The White House, in the White House Office of Management and Budget, as Special Assistant to the Director, Office of Management and Budget,

without the guidance, mentorship, direction, and support, of Pierpont Mobley, whom President Carter had named as his very first White House Diversity Chief.

"Not all people embraced young professionals; not all people embraced African American professionals; not all people embraced women professionals. I was all of the above.

"I quickly learned that not all people were kind or decent. Not all people approved or applauded the hiring of a young, black woman, with little or no professional experience, (one of the youngest to ever have worked at The White House at that time). Some looked at this with utter distain and disbelief, and made their positions known. I also quickly learned that not all people were fair, and unbiased, like President Jimmy Carter. Some made it their daily mission to let me know their feelings...by their words and actions.

With the support of the President, Ham Jordan, Bert Lance, and Jim McIntyre, Pierpont Mobley was always there to resolve or rectify any given situation I was confronted, allowing me, and others like me, to professionally grow, to learn, and blossom professionally, and with confidence."

-Raymone K. Bain
Founder/Chairman, The Raymone K. Bain Companies, LLC

~~~~~~

Testimonial for our dear friend, Pierpont

Congratulations Pierpont on this milestone accomplishment! We've heard you talk about writing a book, on your life, over the years. Indeed, this book is another item you can add to your impressive list of achievements!

We treasure our friendship with you and your family that spans well over 40 years. During that time, your kind, caring nature, and intellect has been self-evident. Qualities, we're sure, that helped make you successful in the equal employment opportunity arena, a sought-after political advisory, and your many other endeavors.

Well done our dear friend.

Magruder and Andrea Murray

My Testimony for a very good friend:

My wife told me recently that Pierpont has finally finished writing his book, so I guess I need to testify on his behalf. From my own perspective, he has been a truly successfully and a good family man.

Years ago, both of my uncles, Paul and John crew up with Pierpont Mobley, here in DC. They served papers together in northeast DC. Moreover, he has been a dear friend and somewhat of a mentor of mine for many years. He informed me that he has decided to write the book about the many years he was employed at the White House under four Presidents. Years ago, he told me what he had to go through there since he was the only black in the personnel office of about 30 employees.

As a retired Command Sergeant Major for the DC National Guards, we have been friends for many years. As he was also a retired Sergeant First Class member of the DC Guard also. Therefore, he played a role in my career along with my family. He has always been a very respectful individual and he has always been trying to help others while he dealt with civil and human rights. As I recall, he was always volunteering for something and became very much involved in DC politics after retiring from the federal government. His character and skills in working with others have always been an asset in his long career.

I am delighted to give a good word for a real friend.

SMC Herman (Rip) Preston

A testimony from a childhood friend:

I was recently informed that Pierpont was writing a book on his many years in EEO and human rights. Therefore, I am elated to provide this on his behalf:

I could not resist making this statement about my childhood friend that came up in our Northeast neighborhood. I, along with Pierpont and Otis, another friend decided to enlist into the DC National guards because we were all interested in receiving a quarterly paycheck from them. Later, I decided to go into the Marines, however, he chose to stay into the DC National Guards along with several of our friends. We all wanted to duck the military draft since we had graduated from high school and were not attending college. Back then, you were subject to be drafted once we had graduated from high school. While he was in the Guard, as a senior NCO, he wrote several Affirmative Action Reports for the DOA and played a role as a race relations coordinator. He was also a Military Policeman.

Pierpont and I both graduated later from Antioch Law School during the same period while both of us were working for the Federal Government. As I recall, he attended night school on a part time basis 9 (nine) years before he received his graduate degree.

I take a lot pride regarding his service at the White House for so many years because a home boy in there was history for our neighborhood. He was very active in Blacks in Government (BIG) and was known for standing up when our folks were being discriminated against therefore, folks were aware that he was the only African American to be selected in the Personnel Office. He would often tell me of the many instances where whites were treating blacks and some females in a discriminated manner, but he often found ways to intervene when he could without being fired himself.

Although we were in EEO at different agencies before retiring, Pierpont always was well thought of and played a very important role in making sure our folks were being treated with respect in equal opportunity employment.

Charles Henson, JD, MLS

~~~~~~

I had the distinct pleasure of meeting Mr. Pierpont Mobley in 1972 when I became a new employee at The White House. This was the Administration of President Richard Nixon. Pierpont was a Personnel Specialist at The White House. He was well-versed, and I mean well-versed, with the rules and regulations as set forth by the Office of Personnel Management (OPM). I desperately needed the advice of a seasoned personnel advisor when I encountered an issue with a personal matter. Pierpont overheard me speaking with another staffer in his office and didn't hesitate to intervene to fix my problem. Pierpont was not afraid to step out to help where needed.

Pierpont can be described as a knowledgeable speaker (can speak on any subject), a kind spirit, full of laughter and a fashionable dresser. Once you meet Pierpont you will never forget him! I am proud to have had that opportunity and I thank God that we recently reconnected after so many years apart.

Shirley Key Ballard, worked for The White House from 1972-1982 as a Secretary/Administrative Assistant in the Nixon Administration.

Uncle Mo,

What can we say? This book is timely and yet, overdue! Certainly, this limited space could never capture the breadth and depth of what you mean to us or how much you have poured into our lives.

We are so proud of your accomplishments! First, as a strong Black Man. Your brand of manhood is so needed in our community! You are the leader of your family - and that word family, like the word father, extends far beyond the nuclear. We call you Uncle Mo, but "father" is an honor that you selflessly extend to us all. You advise, admonish and you love all of us through our best and worst of times. You have a knack of seeing the best in people and inspiring and motivating them to become their best; and we remember the words you speak into our lives.

You are a warrior for justice and your passion for equity and equality for all people is legendary and historical! We love listening to your stories and looking at the photographs of you with all those dignitaries and important people, but mostly, we love being in your presence! In many of those photos, you're the only African American man among a sea of white faces. We marvel at how you could survive and thrive in that environment and still emerge on the other side intact and with the same humility and fervor for humanity.

A man of valor, wit, humor, integrity and intelligence. How did we get so lucky to be part of your legacy? We could not be prouder and more honored to call you Uncle Mo.

Now, the whole world will know why- and not a moment too soon!

We love you to the moon and back and "there's nothing that you can do about it!"

Sincerely,

Sonya Mull and all the other nieces and nephews – too many to name!

~~~~~~

Congratulations to my good friend Pierpont on finally getting his book published!

I've known him for close to 50 years and been close to him thru thick and thin. Pierpont is consistent in his friendship and I have always been able to count **on** him for good advice and a helping hand.

Pierpont is a good example of the perfect family man and a great father figure to his own kids as well as other young people. He is also a wonderful community worker that many count on for good information and he has a kind heart when it comes to others that may be in need of consolation and support.

I can't wait to read the book!

HELLO!!!!!!!!

Richard Lee,
CEO and Chairman
Lee's Flower Shop

~~~~~~

"A fearless fighter, Pierpont Mobley is the man you want in your corner when going up against the government establishment. Being in despair with my unjust/unfair employment removal, Pierpont stuck by my side, encouraging me to see the light that we had a strong case, and we were going to win. And win we did! His in-depth knowledge of human rights law, government policies, along with his strategic negotiation skills allowed me not only return to my original work grade but receive back pay and all entitlements. Absolutely first-rate, he is a resilient defender, and dedicated to his clients cause..."

I wish Pierpont good luck with his writing and look forward to getting an autographed copy of his book.

K. Walker

~~~~~~

I am so glad to know that Mr. Mobley is writing a book on his work experiences in civil rights. I wanted take this opportunity to share my experience because he was instrumental in winning my case against my employer and he assisted me in getting another job.

I had been a supervisor for more than 8 years, but because I questioned several management practices, my manager fired me. I was referred to Mr. Mobley by co-workers who knew of his reputation and told me that he helped individuals with little or no money with the idea he would get paid for his experience and time if he won my case. He represented me during my appeal with EEOC and the Office of Administrative Hearings.

After three years of persistence and lending his legal expertise, Mr. Mobley resolved my discrimination case with reinstatement and retroactive back pay. He was truly a blessing to me and has been to others because his passion and commitment to civil and human rights.

I want to be one of the first ones to purchase his book!

E. Carey

If gives me pleasure to send a congratulatory message to my dear friend, Pierpont Mobley on the publishing of his book.

For more than 25 years after he retired from the government, we became great friends through the DC political arena. He was involved in facilitating several mayoral and council campaigns and his unique leadership style was often inspiring to me, as a political individual and others on the team. As a Manager for the Washington Gas Company who also engaged with the community, I was aware of his great reputation throughout the community because of his volunteerism on various city human rights projects. He was later appointed to our Board at WG and still serves on it for more than 7 years.

Even today, he continues to volunteer in our city focusing on mentoring our young black men and boys.

I am pleased to have the opportunity to express my best wishes on the release of his book.

F. Patterson

~~~~~~

"Quick-witted, smart, friendly, and handsome, in a sea of white faces, it was heaven to see a person of color greet me when I first stepped foot into the White House. While serving in three Presidential Administrations (Johnson, Nixon, Carter), he helped me navigate complicated processes to a successful White House career." I wish Pierpont all the best on the release of his book!

Carole Jones Mumin

I had the opportunity to work on several social programs with my friend, Pierpont back in the day. At the time, he was still employed as a senior level manager with USDA. I was aware that he was dedicated to equal employment opportunity and human rights causes and that he volunteered his time with various workforce development projects and on the Luke C Moore Academy School Board for years.

It was well known across the city that if you had a question about EEO, sexual or workplace harassment, he was the " go to man."

I also recall that he and his wife Jeannette were instrumental in helping the late Dr. Janette Hoston Harris and others in establishing the Washington DC Hall of Fame which has recognized and honored over a 20 year period DC residents that have played significant roles in the betterment of our city. I was blessed to be honored by this esteemed group.

My congratulatory note is made on behalf of a black man whom considers himself a "Peacemaker," and by all his works and actions this is true.

I look forward to reading about his experiences working in the White House under four different Presidents. We salute and congratulate Pierpont on the release of his book.

Charles (Chuck) Hicks
Founder & Director
Black History Celebration Committee

Pierpont Mobley, a true Renaissance man! So, you finally have gotten your book written. Congratulations!

We know this achievement was supported by your lifelong partner Jeannette who introduced my wife Ellen and I to you over 50 years ago in her hometown of Uniontown. Pa. What we both noticed about you was that you were a gentleman who met no strangers. You were comfortable with yourself, self - confident, but not cocky, and you showed us that you liked and respected Jeannette. Our first impressions were spot on, as evidenced by a marriage that has thrived and strengthened for over fifty-five years!

We have been friends and supporters of each other, and our friendship has seen the growth of our children and grandchildren. What a mighty God we serve. Pierpont, we congratulate you on the professional life and successful civil rights career you have achieved that has led to your writing a book that will leave a legacy for your children, grandchildren and generations to come.

Blessings and Peace to you both from our Lord and Savior Jesus Christ,

Rev. Dr. Hiawatha and Ellen Fountain & Family

~~~~~~

Congratulations to Pierpont on the writing of his book. We are proud of his accomplishment and know our family members in S Carolina are beaming with pride.

Pierpont used his passion and experience in EEO and Civil Right to help so many people both in his jobs and those who sought his help in the community.

He had the good fortune of successfully working under 4 Presidents from both parties. His expertise, perseverance, personality and ability to handle conflicts to a successful resolution made him the right person for the job.

Cousin,
Windy Carson Smith, Esq.

~~~~~~

Mr. Mobley told me a few years back that he was going to write a book about his White House days. I told him that I wanted to be sure he included my testimony I sent in advance, of his much appreciated support of me and my fellow colleagues who worked in the Administrative and Messenger units.

During the 1970's, I was detailed from a defense agency at the White House as a Courier/Messenger in the Office of Administration.

Mr. Mobley was known to us as the only black in the Personnel Office. He had a reputation of being fair, getting employees issues resolved and fighting for us to get promotions like our fellow white employees during the Nixon and Ford administrations.

We also had to seek Mr. Mobley's assistance when we would have issues arise with some of the Nixon and Ford staffers. In Mr. Mobley's position, he was instrumental in helping so many, not just blacks, but anyone who needed his help. He surely will always be remembered as a "stand-up guy."

Reverend James Kilby, Posthumously

Contents

Chapter 1

Preface

I am Pierpont Morgan Mobley, a name you are unlikely to encounter again. I entered this world at Freedman's Hospital in Washington, DC, without the advantages of privilege. My mother went into labor prematurely, leaving my parents without an agreed-upon name. It was a nurse at the hospital who suggested naming me Pierpont Morgan, after the renowned banker and financier John Pierpont Morgan, Jr., who was also a philanthropist and followed in his father's footsteps. The junior Morgan passed away in 1943, yet the JP Morgan Chase brand continues to serve millions of customers and businesses today. However, as I mentioned, I was not one of the lucky ones born with a "golden spoon."

The concept for this book was created many years ago when I decided to reflect on the many challenges I have been involved in as a *Peacemaker*. I think my first motivation to engage in the practice of inquiry, resolution and peacemaking came into my consciousness around the age of 11. I recall playing football in our neighborhood in Northwest, D6 with Willie Wood of Bay Packers. I remember missing the pass because the football was thrown too high and landed across the street. To retrieve it, I had to go on the other side of the street, the side where we were told was reserved for whites only. When I went to retrieve the ball, a white man hollered at me and told me *"Get that ball and go back where you came from!"* At the age of 11, I just did not understand what had happened to make him talk to me that way.

Now, decades later, I am well aware that no one has the right to ever talk that way to me.

There were several motivations for this book; The primary one is to tell a story that is replete with history and an understanding of how the Presidential Administrations, and other government agencies, have navigated the pressing issues of race in America through an unrestrictive lens. Over the course of 50 years, I have witnessed many historic benchmarks, sometimes being in the middle of it, and sometimes on the bench. However, the most important thing is to tell our stories, the way it was. While I was employed at the White House for more than 16 years, I was told often that our government was the pillar of democracy. *I must say, it was a **privilege** for working there all those years.* However, democracy, as we learned in the civics classes, had nuances of application, particularly for my people.

This was quite apparent with the contemporary elections, and how we as Black people in this country continue to battle our way through this paradigm we call "white supremacy". The stark realities came to light with the Obama presidency followed by the antithesis, "DT 45" (Trump). On Obama's first day in office, he was confronted by several white republican congressional officials letting him know that his Administration was "doomed" from the start, which was clearly racially motivated on its face. I don't remember ever reading that any other President, in the past, had ever received such a "welcoming." I don't believe with his Harvard status he was prepared for this direct hostility of disparate treatment!

As a black professional mediator and civil and human rights facilitator, for more than 40 years, it was a challenge. I was angered by the stark disparities often displayed in this country.

From my experience, the Administration was not exempt from discrimination. They often had to deal with mean-spirited remarks, racial disputes, stereotypes, and other matters related to race, sex, age, disabilities and sexual orientation, etc. that were flagrantly displayed in the workplace. I was constantly challenged with maintaining the tenets of being an effective mediator and "Peacemaker". This story begins with my ancestors who, as people of African descent, always were striving to maintain peace in their homes and communities. Back in those days, it seems their strengths were applied through self-confidence and togetherness. However, the family unit was often challenged in order to stay focused on family safety and racism.

In today's environment, it appears that hateful behavior is more acceptable than dealing with those promoting goodwill treatment for one another. Therefore, my wisdom tells me that our peacemaking efforts are not being realized as it should be so. We must begin to make peace with signs of equity, inclusion, diversity tolerance, and acceptance if we wish to maintain this *"Good Trouble"* for a period of time.

Chapter 2

The Great Migration

I t was in the dark of night when they left, my parents, older brothers, and sister. The story was that they planned their exodus from Saluda, South Carolina from the sharecropping farm where they picked cotton. My mother (Geneva Lott) and father (Moses Mobley), both had 7th grade educations, and never talked about the conditions or the horrors they experienced. I can only imagine their journey, like so many others, to head north from the naked oppression of the South.

In my later years, I learned that many Black people participated in a historic event, the *Great Migration*, where over 6 million African Americans left the tyrannical conditions of the South and headed North, West and Midwest. It was the largest migration recorded in the history of the US. Many came to Washington, D.C., where I was born and raised. Our Ancestors all *carried* but did not tell of the toxic oppression they witnessed.

There was never any profit for those who worked on the land sharecropping, as my parents did. The system of sharecropping, for many African Americans, was a sequel to plantation life. After the Civil War, the absence of cash or an independent credit system led to its creation. High interest rates, unpredictable harvests, and unscrupulous landlords and merchants often kept tenant farm families severely indebted. These actions required the debt to be carried over until the next year or the next.

Laws favoring landowners made it difficult or even illegal for sharecroppers to sell their crops to others besides their landlord. Akin to slavery, the laws fostered perpetual indebtedness and tethered people to poverty. [1]

The Great Migration, resulted in the loss of free or cheap labor for many white landowners, who often resorted to accomplices in law enforcement to arrest and confine many African Americans. Many were arrested on the train platform when they tried to leave to head north. It is only destiny that my parents made it onto that train and traveled through several southern states so that they could breathe their way to a better life.[2]

Not knowing the stories...the details, is something that I subconsciously felt and used to my advantage to survive later in life. Further, it enriched my perspective of the staunch resilience of my mother, father, grandparents, and all those that came before me. Most of them were sharecroppers out of South Carolina.

Many folks like mine escaped from the Jim Crow suppressive environment to seek better opportunities in the North. In our case, I was told that several of my mother's relatives were in the "Big" D.C. They felt safe coming to the nation's capital where they could find housing and other comforts. When we got here, they told me that my mother was pregnant with me and were surrounded by at least three of her brothers and one sister. Moreover, my father later told us that he had to leave down there to escape being killed by the whites because he just did not like the way they were treated in Saluda. He often said that the white man just did not care for the blacks or their welfare. My father would go on to tell us they were treated like they were nothing!

Chapter 3

Night Sticks, Churches, and Northeast

As indicated earlier, my family came to Washington, D.C. in 1937 amid the Great Depression and two years shy of WWII. I am the 4th fourth child of Geneva and Moses Mobley. I was the youngest of four children, and the only one born in Washington, D.C. Being the youngest of my one sister and two brothers, I was given the name *"Pap"*. Growing up for me in our neighborhood was one with radio's blaring the latest songs to which we would dance and have large Sunday dinners. Family was very important. We went to our neighborhood school and life at that young age felt to be seamless.

During the early years, our family moved around in a 12-block radius from our initial home. We were often warned by our parents that we were not to wander all over the neighborhood.

My parents often expressed fear of us being kidnapped by whites and other dangerous folks. As part of our training in a racist world, we were told that white folks were devils, to never look straight into a white's eyes, and by no means argue with them for fear of retaliation, particularly in the workplace. The teachings of our parents were tinted with the realities of living in a segregated D.C. in the 30's and 40's and the Jim Crow south. Although D.C. was known as the epicenter for federal jobs and a hub for cultural and academic organizations, segregation and racism dictated our progress. There were always incidents of conflict between the races and one thing we learned early on was to avoid conflict with white people.

Washington had relatively few "Jim Crow" laws, however, segregation and racism were endemic. The few existing laws mandated integration in the public schools and recreation facilities, but not on the streetcars and public libraries.   It was the backdrop of these historical events that heightened the need for prayer. So, it is only fitting that we went to church, and prayed a lot– hoping things would get better for my mother and father, who both had to work while my brothers and sister attended nearby schools. Going to church was a normal Sunday thing, folks in my neighborhood attended Southern Baptist Church off New Jersey Avenue, NW. I still remember uttering the following, "We *bind you Satan, and every menacing spirit that would stir up against God's people in Jesus' name.* Being close to the Lord was a daily thing for Black people and prayer was a fixture of our culture and our salvation.

Our parents sacrificed a lot of family time and worked long hours to provide for us. My father, Moses Mobley, worked two jobs, he was a construction worker and often worked part-time at Featherstone Gas Station, on New Jersey Avenue, NW. My mother and father worked as a team, to achieve the dream of getting a larger house in a better neighborhood. Mother took courses at Apex Beauty School on U Street, NW, to become a licensed beautician and eventually worked at a salon on 11 Street, NE. This learned behavior while in my youth, encouraged me to always "keep the peace." She became well known for the way she "did hair", particularly among the sisters at church. She put in a lot of hours to help provide for the family.   With their hard work, we eventually moved away from New Jersey Avenue to 13th Street, N.E. Back then, this area was considered a better neighborhood. My parents, with their 7th grade educations, were savvy enough to save and invest in a larger home in an area which was known for better schools. We attended church every Sunday, so we knew that God would continue to bless our family because the move enhanced our family educational opportunities. Although it took a lot of savings, our mother was sure that our God would continue to bless us. When we purchased in 1950, about five months after, my father had a stroke and basically bead-ridden until he died seven years later.

In addition to prayer, we also had the "Council of Elders" in our respective neighborhood(s) that served as guides and mentors to the younger folks in the community. My personal mentor was Mr. Enoch Gray who would prove to be the one person who gave me an opportunity that led to so many other roads in my life. Mr. Gray stepped in as a father figure when my father became ill and eventually passed. I will always honor the words of wisdom he gave to me.

The "elders" understood all too well what barriers we faced with racism, as they had experienced it five-fold themselves. We would often be admonished for things that might bring harm to ourselves or our families. I was often told by my parents and "elders" about ways to avoid the police and jail. Although it did not keep us all out of jail or from pursuing the wrong path, many of us listened to their counsel and steered clear of the infamous D.C. jail. People often told stories of instances of being in the right place at the wrong time. These experiences were not unfamiliar to the Black community. The ongoing harassment of the Black community was a favorite pastime of the police; and many of the officers were black!

Oppressive encounters with the D.C. police were prevalent throughout my childhood and into adulthood. Dating back to 1936, the Washington chapter of the National Negro Congress organized and protested police brutality and segregation in recreation areas because of the unlawful violence and oppression by law enforcement was routine. Ironically, some

80 years later, Black organizations and Black people are still protesting and filing charges against law enforcement due to the harassment and blatant killing of our people. Since the founding of this country, negative encounters with some type of law enforcement are common among Black folks, particularly young Black males.

When I was growing up, most black males thought twice before going out alone at night, and parents were reluctant to let their sons walk around unattended.

I always pray with joy...being confident of this, that he who began a good work in you will carry it on to completion until the day of Christ Jesus.

-Philippians 1:4-6

My negative experiences with law enforcement are still embedded in my mind. I remember the night sticks, threats and being called the N word; In some ways it prepared me for what was to come.

These memories would also take me back to the past, wondering what my parents and all my family from the South must have endured, and what they never talked about. They often were very quiet when these issues would come up.

Chapter 4

Pool Halls, Integration & Dirty Hands

I was not a good student. I loved hanging out at the pool room and honing my skills as a professional pool player. I never saw myself at this point in life of being someone who would engage in anything too serious. I had visions of my second home being a smoky pool hall, hanging out with the guys, and making some change. Although most folks thought I was pretty good, my young mind did not understand the practice and professionalism of such things. In the interim, school kind of lingered; I did not take education as seriously during those days. I had my fill of the classroom as I began to understand disparities and how we as Black folk were getting the burnt end of life.

I came home from the pool hall one day and my father was waiting for me in the living room. Dad was in a wheelchair due to a stroke; he told me that I was to transfer to Eastern High School because of integration. I was confused because I was prepared to go to McKinley where I already attended for 4 days (it was the beginning of the school year). As it turns out, I had to go to Eastern because we lived on the east side of North Capitol Street.

I did not know exactly what I was in for and took the news without much enthusiasm. This was around 1955. The push for integration, resulting from Brown vs Board of Education, was the beginning of all of this. Schools were mandated to integrate.

I had heard about some of the other schools across the country that were attempting to integrate, it was violently protested by whites who wanted to maintain the status quo.

What many people do not know, is that the case of Brown v Board of Education was a combination of 5 cases: Brown, Briggs v Elliott (South Carolina), Davis v County School Board of Prince Edward County (Virginia), Gebhart v Belton (Delaware), and Bolling v Sharpe (Washington, D.C.). Back then, I did not appreciate the fact that I was a part of history. Because of my academic training in law, I found the case history of D.C. particularly interesting because I "lived" the experience. Many people who lived outside of D.C. had the impression that Washington, D.C. was progressive and did not have harsh problems with segregation similar to the South. However, the opposite existed.

Between 1930 and 1950 (in part due to the Great Migration), the Black population in the District of Columbia doubled, and federal government job opportunities for African Americans became available due to the New Deal program of the 1930s. This was coupled with opportunities for African Americans in the service sectors and skilled markets. The increase in the African American population was accompanied by an increase in the Black student population, from 33 percent to 50 percent. Overcrowding in Black schools worsened in the District as World War II halted school construction.

Between 1941 and 1947 about 10 percent of the Black student population went on double or even triple shifts to attend school, while White schools had rooms to spare. School administrators planned to construct new schools for the long-term, but as an immediate, fix 21 all-White schools were turned to all-Black schools. This was resented by White parents for "taking away" their designated schools. Similarly, Black parents were resentful, they had a problem with the action(s) of city government as they viewed the move with the additional schools as "hand-me-downs."[3]

All this served as a backdrop to a historical act by the Consolidated Parents Group, Inc. In 1947, they began a crusade to end segregated schooling in Washington, D.C. They petitioned the school board (C Melvin Sharpe was the head of the School Board) to use Sousa Junior High School on an integrated basis, as it could adequately offer Anacostia pupils a full Junior High program without additional cost for repairs or construction. This action would serve all the students and would not be subject to overcrowding.

On September 11, 1950, in a carefully planned maneuver, the head of the Consolidated Parent's Group, along with student Spottswood Bolling and 11 other Black school children, presented themselves at the newly constructed Sousa School for admission along with a "police escort and a battery of lawyers." The principal refused to admit the children. The denial led Bolling and the other students to begin their school year at Shaw Junior High, a 48-year-old school, ill-equipped, with a playground too small for a ball field, a welding shop turned into a makeshift gymnasium, and science lab with a Bunsen burner and a bowl of goldfish.[4]

Although there were stark differences in the integrity of the schools, James Nabrit, Jr. law professor from Howard University, did not present evidence that schools the plaintiffs attended were inferior to the facilities for white students. Although it was a risky position, he felt the sole issue was that of segregation itself. The U.S. District court dismissed the case based on a recent ruling by the Court of Appeals in *Carr v. Corning*, that segregated schools were constitutional in the District of Columbia. Nabrit filed an appeal and was waiting for a hearing when the U.S. Supreme Court sent word that it was interested in considering the case along with the other four segregation cases already pending. The U.S. Supreme Court rendered a separate opinion on *Bolling v. Sharpe* based on the Fifth Amendment because the Fourteenth Amendment to the U.S. Constitution was not applicable in the District of Columbia.[56]

Everything that was cited in the court case was more than just integration, it was reality regarding the environment and real-world disparities between White vs Black schools. Eastern and Armstrong were textbooks for the word "disparity", a tale of two schools.

So here I was, wedged into the wave of integration of D.C. public schools. Although I do not remember all the details, I distinctly remember having some trepidation to attend Eastern. All of this was made worse as I was escorted by a police officer every day for the first couple of weeks, to ensure my entry into the school. The first day of being escorted by the policeman, I kept a distance from the officer. My heart was racing, I just knew that there would be hundreds of screaming white parents in front of the school, reminiscent of the "Little Rock Nine" in Arkansas. However, when I got there, there was little fanfare going on. All I remember was that it was eerily quiet and routine during my enrollment at Eastern for a history-making event.

My first impression about Eastern is that it was clean, it had clean walls, hallways, and chandeliers. The school was very large and clean, it was like a new school, even though Eastern had been around for years. The look of Eastern was a stark contrast to my middle school Langley and Armstrong High located across town in the Black community with a crumbling infrastructure and dark halls.

Naturally, we (Black students) were not accepted nor treated in a civilized fashion at Eastern. It was so hard to study because there was always that fear that something was going to happen...feeling as though you could be maimed or killed. Well, those concerns did not go unfounded. On my third day at Eastern, while walking down the hall, a white girl stabbed my schoolmate, Harold Jackson in the leg. She then ran out of the school, jumped into a car, and was hastily driven away. Not long after that incident, a young black female student asked me why I even bothered to try to attend Eastern since the Whites did not want us there.

She then warned us that "we needed to watch out for that red Volkswagen" on the corner because some white boys were probably up to no good. Just two days later the police raided the car and found over 20 weapons, the White boys went to jail. Due to this incident, and many others (which are probably locked in the recesses of my mind), many of the Black students left Eastern before the year was over. It was the opinion of my parents not to run away from the problems at Eastern, so I stayed there for a year and half before enrolling in Armstrong High School.

Ironically, there is one person I remember at Eastern more than anyone else, Mr. Pierce. Mr. Pierce was a teacher at Eastern, he was Black, according to the census. However, Mr. Pierce was light skinned, carried himself as if he was white, and was an all-out racist.

He often made racist remarks about Black people in class and routinely made fun of us in front of the all-white students in his class. It was like a page out of the Soldier's Story! He was very mean and condescending to us. My first encounter with him he told the Black kids in class that he did not want us to tear up "his" school. Mr. Pierce then directed all the Black students to sit in the back of the room and he would give us a "C", if we *did not* participate in class, just turn in our papers and be quiet. Mr. Pierce and others like him remind me of those who not only despise the fact that they are Black, but also have played a role of being a detriment to our progress, willing to do whatever it takes to debilitate their own people.

I often remember wanting to retaliate against him in some way. Little did I know then that the stars would align, and I would be able to get my revenge in the sweetest way.

I saw Mr. Pierce about 25 years later walking down Pennsylvania Avenue near the White House. When I recognized him, I made a beeline to speak. When I said, "Hello Mr. Pierce", he appeared afraid and bothered at the same time. I advised him of who I was and that he looked like my former teacher at Eastern High. Once he acknowledged that he was Mr. Pierce, everything spilled out. I told him I was surprised to see him again and I wanted him to know that his actions toward the Black students at Eastern back in the day were distasteful, particularly to the males in the class. Further, he demonstrated discriminatory behavior in the classroom, and it inspired me to seek graduate level training in the area(s) of civil and human rights. During this mini tirade, we approached the White House gate. I stopped and told him that I had been a Senior White House Personnel Specialist for the past 16 years and, in some ways, I had him to thank for that. Mr. Pierce looked perplexed as I began to walk through the White House gate, greeted by Secret Service. As I turned around to him to impart last words, he looked with his mouth hanging open, "Thank You so much Mr. Pierce!". I then looked toward the Heavens and thanked God I was able to get that man back in some way, not only for me, but for the countless other Black students that had been exposed to his malice.

After eighteen months of dipping in and out of school, I eventually transferred to Armstrong Technical High[7], so that I could graduate the following year.

I had lost almost a year of school because my family was afraid that I might get hurt due to all the hostilities and violence that came with the first wave of integration. When I transferred to Armstrong, I could see the stark differences in how the "system" valued the education of Black students.

Armstrong had dirty walls, no updated equipment, broken-down seats, same old cafeteria; it seemed that the city was never interested in giving us environmental parity, like the White schools, like Eastern. Thinking back, I know we had some great and dedicated teachers and counselors at Armstrong. They worked with the least equipment and resources to make things better for our community. Often, they had to use their own money to assist us in preparing for life endeavors, such as tuition or vocational training, as well as any other assistance that we needed going into adulthood. Ironically, many things that our teachers did back then at Armstrong are the same things that teachers are doing today in our urban schools. Often having to pay money for students so they would have the necessities to have a valued educational experience; or getting grants to provide the type of access that is needed to prepare them for academics and occupations. The disparities continue to exist as not too much has changed in the past 65 years.

Patriots, Payback & Purpose

I was in the Army Reserves for 20 years; I joined at the age of 19 during my senior year of high school. It's strange how sometimes fate has a way of guiding your path. I was walking down the hallway at Eastern and happened to see a sign for recruitment into the Reserves. It was there I met John Fields, a Second Lieutenant and recruiter for District of Columbia National Guard (DCNG), who'd come to Eastern on his rounds to different D.C. schools. Fields took out time to talk with me. Although I am not one to outwardly discuss my personal business, for some reason I shared with him my challenges at the time: the pressure to make some extra money to help my mother as my father had just died and we had to keep our home. Mr. Fields suggested that I join the National Guard (DCNG) as a part-time job. He further explained the benefits of being in the military. At that moment, I decided to join the Reserves and begin basic training. The reserves gave me an opportunity to broaden my perspective of the world and learn how to deal with other cultures. Throughout my more than 20 years as a reservist, I achieved the rank of Sergeant First Class (E-7).

While in the Reserves, I wore many hats and worked for different departments. I gained experience writing several Affirmative Action Reports for the Department of the Army. I also dabbled in recruitment by actively engaging and recruiting other females into the military. I guess I was what they call a Diversity Specialist today. I was also a human resource supervisor, a Supply Supervisor and a Race Relations Specialist during my tenure.

The decision to join and stay in the Reserves was one of the best decisions I ever made. The military was my first opportunity to understand discipline, human rights, leadership, and cultural awareness; all which led me to devote my life to a human and civil rights career. Although I never took my studies seriously, my military experience exposed me to avenues where I was motivated to seek additional degrees and opportunities. This mindset was a step away from working various service jobs and hanging out at the pool hall. In retrospect, I think I started to take life more seriously, especially since I attended four HS before graduating.

I thought that being in the Reserves would give me some type of protective shield from being harassed by the police, but it did not work out that way. Even though we lived in a different neighborhood, there was still no reprieve from getting involved with D.C. police.

Ironically, I applied for a position with the D.C. Police Department since the Reserves was just part-time/occasional weekend duty. After changing tires at Stidham Tire Company for 4 years, I wanted to do something else with better pay. During the interview with D.C. Police, I was instructed in front of a selection panel to give reasons why I had been involved in several police disputes that led to being charged with two disorderly conduct violations. I had to explain to the panel (1 white male, 1 black male, and a white female) why they should select me for the force despite having a poor record with them already. So, I had to describe the following incidents that lead up to those "violations":

In the first instance, I had just finished my after-school job of setting up pins at Greenway Bowling Alley. My friend, Otis and I stopped by the Little Tavern Restaurant, who was famous for having good hamburgers on Minnesota Avenue and Benning Road. While we were purchasing two hamburgers, here were two young white females sitting in one of the booths. I was wearing my Armstrong High School sweater on. They started to engage me in conversation about where I went to school and how they liked my sweater. During our conversation, two white police officers came in and told Otis and I that we had to leave immediately. We said we were only waiting on our hamburgers we had just ordered before they entered. As usual back in those days, police would go in back to take breaks or something. After about three minutes, the policemen jumped over the counter and put us in handcuffs. They then marched us four blocks to Precinct 14. The white officers claimed that we were disorderly and charged us Disorderly Conduct. Both girls began to laugh as we were being handcuffed and taken to the police station. We had not done anything to deserve this type of racist harassment. After explaining to my mother why we were charged, she told the officers there that we did nothing to be placed in jail for. Without holding her tongue, I believe I heard her say, "this was all about race, and they would get theirs." She paid the $5.00 fine and took me home. The second time I was arrested was when I was on my way home with a bunch of my friends. It was about ten of us, all around our late teens. We were all walking down Florida Avenue toward 13th St, NE around 11:30 pm. With all the group bantering back in forth we did not notice the police car pull up. Before we knew it, two white officers jumped out of their vehicle and approached us. They looked as though they were ready to bust some heads and aggressively told us that someone on 9th & K Streets had complained that we were making too much noise. They immediately pulled out their guns, threatened us, corralled us like a herd of cattle, called a paddy wagon, and took us all to jail. Unfortunately, I was just over 18 years of age, so my mother had to pay another $5.00 to get me released from the jail block.

The third time that comes to mind was an incident with a female friend from Haiti. I met her at Howard University while I was taking Saturday classes for small business. At this time in my life, I was in my early 20's and had just come back from my weekend stint at the Reserves. I was so proud of being in the military. When I first met her, she appeared to be a woman of good character, well educated, and was a Pharmacy student at Howard University. Although we were basically good friends and had gone out a few times, I wanted to see what Mom

thought of her so I took her by the house. Although Mom was cordial, she told me that my friend was "too light", a foreigner, and she hoped I was not thinking of anything serious with her.

One night we were driving down Bladensburg Road. I had borrowed my mother's car to take my friend back home around 11:00 p.m. I was so busy talking and trying to be cool, I did not notice that we had slowly passed a police car with two white officers. Apparently when the police peered into the car, they noticed that my friend was light skinned, and they thought she was white. Unknown to me, they immediately turned around, pulled us over, and parked right in front of us. They threw a bright spotlight that glared through the windshield. I could not see anything, I put my hands up over my eyes to shield my eyes from the light.   My friend was talking but I could not hear her because my heart was beating so hard. In keeping with the narrative of a Black man being the chauffeur and the white person riding in the back, they asked me to get out and step away from the car. I told the policeman that I was in the military reserves (for some reason, I thought that would make a difference). The guy told me to "shut up", put my hands up and to lean up against the car while they cuffed my hands behind my back. They then went to her side to inspect her ethnicity or something. Once they realized that she was not "white - white", they still wanted to make the point, so they grabbed me (without stating cause), and took me to jail just to show her that they had power over me. They released me within an hour. I believed my friend's folks, who were Haitian diplomats, may have called the precinct to get me released before I was taken to the cell block and there was an international incident.

Ironically, after all those stories, the police department hired me. Unlike today, the police department's funding by the city was minimal compared to what is budgeted from the city coffers today. They advised me that they did not have enough money to fully train me and other applicants (I do not know whether this was just for the Black police officers or what). If I recall, back then when you were not fully Trained you were sent out with a "half blue/green uniform" as a Policeman Aid until they officially appointed you as officers the next fiscal year.

My first main assignment was to write parking tickets and occasionally direct traffic at 7 & F Street, NW. That turned out to be my only assignment(s) due to what happened to Elmer. My dear friend Elmer Hunter, who joined the police ranks around the same time I did, went through the full training. Elmer had been on his beat for several days. On this occasion, the bus driver stopped, called him over and told him that a person refused to pay to ride the bus. Elmer allegedly called this black man off the bus. The man followed him and as Elmer walked away, the man shot him in the back. The whole incident enraged a lot of people because

Elmer was loved by so many. After that incident, my mother told me at the age of 22, that I had to quit. I had been trained as a Military Police in the Army National Guards, but only half-way trained for the Metropolitan Police Department. I was just there during this five-month period before I accepted the courier position in Ft. Meade, Maryland with the National Security Agency (NSA).

White Privilege, the Feds, Interviews

During my tenure in the Reserves, my "oath" and "duty" were at times tested. I saw how racism permeated every aspect of our lives and led me to question whether the "oath" I took was superficial.

When I enlisted into the D.C. National Guard, I surmised that the military would be a place where everyone would be treated equitably well, I was wrong.

I was exposed to white officers routinely being condescending to the Black officers. After basic training, I was assigned to the 171st MP Battalion as a Race Relations Specialist. I noticed a trend where whites liked to use "God" when they had opportunities to discriminate or torture Black people. Coming from a family who ascribed to the doctrines of the Christian faith, it was so hypocritical. White people would attend church and then come out and hang a Black person, or today, shoot an unarmed Black person. Now how does that go together?

The validity of my oath was questioned when I was first introduced to "real" white privilege. These are things that Black folk would intuitively know but did not have the empirical evidence. I was serving with the D.C. National Guard in the 1960's. I had worked a little way up through the ranks to become a squad sergeant of about 10 enlisted recruits from what I thought was the District. However, as it turns out, many of the recruits were from up and down the East Coast from places like Connecticut, New York and New Jersey, etc.

Although it was not broadcasted, I found out that many of these recruits were eluding the draft and were sons of top white government officials or sons of industry CEO's. Drill dates were once per month, however, many were often excused by the Commanding General with a bevy of explanations for their absences, even though it was supposed to be "mandatory". When they attended, which was seldom, they were never on time. When I complained about this, my captain, who was also white, would tell me that I should just leave them alone. These were privileged white boys ducking the draft.

Believing in the oath I took and understanding how the Reserves worked, I could not imagine, in my naivete, that they (the white recruits) would be able to get away with such things. It took me a while to understand how "exceptions" are made. They all got away with the draft and the reserves. After hearing how former Presidents (like Bill Clinton and George W. Bush) ducked the draft, I realized that this was basically the same thing. They were given a free pass because of their "white privilege." I wanted to discipline them but was instructed to leave them alone.

Maybe the worst stress test of my oath was during the riots of 1968. Immediately after MLK was assassinated in 1968, I was married that same year. My unit (the 171st MP BN, D.C. National Guard) was activated for 15 days. At that time, I held a top-secret clearance from working at the White House. The Commanding General of the DCNG at that time, who was white, assigned me and a white Captain of the Guard to D.C. Police Precinct 7. This precinct was in the NW section of Wisconsin Avenue. There was a lot of rhetoric going on at the time about Stokely Carmichael and the Black Panthers. It was insinuated by the white General more than once that if any Black person, Black Panther, or Stokely was to encroach on

Wisconsin Avenue, there was a standing order of "shoot to kill". So, while the rioting was going on around my mother's beauty shop on H Street, NE, it also expanded all the way over to 14th Street, NW. No one came near the upper Northwest because Blacks knew that this area was totally off-limits.

The riots of 1968 symbolized a clarion call to action. It was not only the reaction to King's assassination, but also the systemic refusal of local and federal government to acknowledge and cease the political, civil and economic injustices that we, as Black people, continued to face generation after generation.

Although D.C. was known as the proverbial *"Chocolate City"*, the District had serious tensions due to labor, economic and housing discrepancies between whites and Blacks.[8] For example, although Black people made up 55 percent of the D.C.'s population in the 60's, they were forced into 44 percent of the city's housing and paid more to get less.[9]

The Washington riots went on for 12 days and resulted in 13 deaths and $24 million in insured property damage.[10] While the mayhem was going on, things were unsettlingly calm up there on Wisconsin avenue. It was a different type of culture that I had not witnessed before. Police officers were treated with admiration; something that I had not experienced in the northeastern part of the city. As a staff sergeant, I noticed that there was only one full-time Black police officer in the entire police station of about 30. When I had the chance to ask, I questioned him about their recruiting practices and not having any other officers that looked like him. I assumed that he would feel uncomfortable being around so many white men with guns. He told me that he did not complain and did not want to "rock the boat" because it felt like *heaven* being assigned to a wonderful post. However, he contradicted himself when he stated that he often heard negative racial jokes and references. He was afraid to complain about them to his supervisor because he did not want to be retaliated against or transferred. Besides, he said, "the whites up there treated him with respect, and he was provided hot coffee and pastries every morning." Ironically, he stated he was finishing up his degree from Howard University.

I eventually left that post after things died down. Often, I thought about the one Black policeman at the precinct; how long he was able to eat pastries and drink the coffee. I never ran into him again. However, he did teach me something about how to get along with others when you were outnumbered in the working environment. Although he was the only black person there, and he accepted his situation by hearing racist statements, and other jokes but he said he maintained his sense of character by speaking up when things got too bad. Moreover, he said they all had to respect him because racial tension was becoming very sensitive throughout the department and the country.

Thinking back on this, I had to use his experiences to prepare myself for possible future encounters. I was also subjected to similar situations while serving the White House as the only black individual in the Personnel Office.

This reminded me how making adjustments in my life after the riots opened many thoughts on how I was going to have to deal with being the only black in an environment where the supervisor did not select me for the position there. Therefore, I had to be ready for a new stressful working environment.

The riots depicted a certain type of fear for me since I was in the reserves. Upon my return to the office, I was abruptly questioned by many white staffers on what my role as was being a sergeant on active duty during this 15-day period. I recall many of the whites were asking me did I have to lock any of the rioters up or did I have to fight anyone? Of course, I had to explain to the entire staff my role as a guardsman in the entire situation.

Chapter 5

1600 Pennsylvania, Avenue, NW

Ft. Meade, the White House, and that Lady

Going back to 1964, my dear mentor and neighbor, Mr. Enoch Gray, suggested that I take the test to work at the National Security Administration (NSA) in Ft. Meade where he worked. I followed his recommendation, passed the test, and was hired. After about 4 months there, I heard an announcement that they wanted two people to work at the White House immediately. I lined up with the other hopefuls and answered a bunch of questions about Washington, D.C., my character, etc. As destiny would have it, I was selected to be detailed to the White House in 1964, soon after the assassination of President John F. Kennedy. In retrospect, I think I was chosen because I already had a high security clearance from being in the Guard. I was on my way to be a courier or analyst next to the White House Situation Room. My title was actually a Clerical Assistant.

Being a courier there was interesting because I got to see different areas and departments at the White House. I was in awe of all the intricacies of the building, the culture; it was a different world than my corner of northeast D.C. Everyone seemed to respect each other. You would see President Lyndon Johnson in the halls with the Secret Service, and he would acknowledge you; all the employees were very friendly. Again, our office was right next to the main Situation Room. As a compliment from the Navy Mess, they would often provide leftovers from various events after the President would go to the mansion for the evening.

My time as a courier consequently led to an appointment in the personnel office since I became very responsive to the Press Office and other top officials.

Both offices would routinely call on me for special projects. Again, as a courier, you were assigned to Administrative Services. Jim Rogers, the Assistant Personnel Officer approached me to share his problem regarding the LBJ Administration getting updates/messages to Congress from the personnel office in a timely manner. Although he did not ask me for a solution per se, I used my initiative to write out the Presidential schedule in coordination with the other departments and the news media. I worked on the problem that next night at home and left the final product on his desk. Jim came to our office that same day and asked who wrote up the new schedule. I told him that I had taken it home and revised it on my own. Rogers could not believe that I took the initiative and was impressed. Soon after the meeting, Mr. Hopkins, the Chief Executive Clerk, approached me. He said he had heard good things about me and was impressed with the schedule I provided for Jim Rogers. Soon after that, Jim Rogers offered me a reassignment for a Personnel Assistant in the White House Personnel Office. I was told by Mr. Hopkins, confidentially, that both he and Rogers "realized" that they needed a Black employee in the office because Martin Luther King had just been killed and they felt this was the right time to select a Black person for the position. Mr. Hopkins advised that there had not been an African American assigned to the personnel office on a permanent basis in the 35 years of his tenure in the White House.

Aside from the death of King, my new appointment was bolstered by my background working on Affirmative Action reports and being a Race Relations Specialist in the Army Reserves.

After the riots, being "sensitive toward affirmative action in the workplace" was in full swing at the Fed level. This promotion, I believed, was fate because Black messengers rarely received promotions there.

Whereas the white employees in the file room and the correspondence unit would know that they would not be looking at the file cabinet too long, before promotions would be coming their way.

At the time of my appointment to the personnel office, I had 13 years of military experience with the D.C. National Guard. It was in the Office where I met "that lady", Jean Robb. She was the Personnel Officer. She presented herself as unassuming, small and wide in stature with a small string of pearls around her neck. She was cautiously welcoming when I came on board, of course as it was the only thing to do. I was the only Black person in the personnel office from 1968 until I left in 1980 during the Carter Administration. My first day, Jean Robb let me know that she had nothing to do with my being in the office. That was the clue that I would be working in a hostile working environment. She then directed me to a desk right by the door, so close that people would hit my desk every time they entered the office (just like the "Spook Who Sat by The Door). Little did I know at the time that would be part of the appetizer course for Jean Robb to neuter my career.

As a youth, Black kids were often told in our respective families, that white folks were devils. Never look them straight in the eyes, and please don't argue with them, for fear of being retaliated against at the workplace. This resonated with me over the years. Well, I heeded NONE of that.

I jumped into my duties; I was very serious about my work because I had to represent my folks. There was always an issue in the personnel office.

As I became more familiar with the routine, more and more people called me for advice and guidance, particularly my Black brothers and sisters. Unknown to me at the time, Jean Robb became more and more agitated with my popularity.

She would openly question among the others in the office, why so many people would call and ask for me, that I must be doing something illegal. Further, Jean Robb would make the typical racist statements in front of the entire staff to goad me into a confrontation such as *"Blacks would never be good leaders because they liked to drive big cars or Black folks like to dance a lot."* In some instances, I would respond to her but usually, I would just avoid her because I knew she was trying to fire me. My position was a political one, which meant I could be fired on the spot, and she reminded me about this on several occasions.

It got so bad that Jean Robb had the secretary and clerk of the office direct all calls to her so that she could see who was calling me and for what. The entire office would laugh at her childish attitude towards me. To add insult to injury, one of her assistants would routinely come over to me to lightly flirt. She would ask me inappropriate things about my clothes, particularly my tie(s), and state how expensive they seemed to be. I was definitely in a "Karen" situation.

If Jean Robb was not enough, some of the white males who came to the office would try to discredit my professional senior position by not addressing me directly. They would speak to the secretary in our office, even though they knew I had the answers to most of their inquiries.

Usually, the white secretary would tell them they would have to talk to me or the other senior specialist. Both secretaries would laugh at them upon their leaving the office.

During this period of coping with Ms. Robb and others, I realized that I had to establish a closer relationship with God. I had been raised in the church and my Mother was a God fearing woman who never missed church. In order to help me cope with the stresses of the job, I recall the scripture from Philippians 4:6, *"Do not be anxious about anything, but in every situation, by prayer and petition, with thanksgiving, present your requests to God."* So, I along with both of my children, joined the Second New St. Paul Baptist Church near our home. The inspiration I received there strengthened my faith, gave me the resolve to take it one day at a time, and to put my situation in a different perspective. I ended up becoming the President of our Youth Fellowship Committee and becoming devoted to the children. Our Youth Church is upstairs and seats at least 50 youths.

Back to the Personnel Office. Being the only Black person in the office was quite the challenge. How dare I be respected and advise people? How dare I have a top-secret clearance and demonstrate the ability to get things done? Despite questions of competency that Black people routinely experience, I was beleaguered with the stereotypical inquiries. For example, I was asked on several occasions, why was I attending college at night because my wife had received a promotion at C and P telephone.[11] I remember my supervisor telling me that since I was a mid-level employee and my wife had been promoted, she would ask, *why were we not satisfied with our incomes? Why did I feel that I would be entitled to a higher GS level? Or, why did we have two cars? Or, we had two children, don't you think that's enough?* Lastly, my favorite, *don't forget to make the coffee or clean the coffee pot before you leave!*

Chapter 6

Second New St.

Paul Baptist

I was always cautioned by management to "stay in my lane" and not become involved in politics. However, as stated previously, I took my job seriously and demonstrated the ability to work well with each Administration. As a result, I was often criticized for my being so visible. Again, I was the only Black person in the office, I had no choice but to be visible. When a human resource issue came up, the political folks would always contact me for assistance. There were many days that I wanted to quit, but I knew Jean Robb was trying to get me out of the office and I was not going to let her "win". Eventually Jean Robb threw down the gauntlet and challenged me to a duel of sorts, and it would change my life.

It was on an occasion when I was on weekend Reserve duty. I was called by Commanding General Bryant, a Black man, who asked me about my job at the White House. He had the impression that I had a senior level position and that it necessitated my leaving the reserves. I was informed that a letter from the White House had been forwarded to the Joint Chiefs of Staff at the Pentagon, and there was some type of deliberation. I was confused, perplexed, and very upset. I found out that Jean Robb had sent a letter to the Joint Chiefs stating that it was best that I be released from the reserves immediately. In truth, I did not have to leave the Reserves. It was not necessary, but whatever she said in that letter, which was sent confidentially, it placed me in a position where I had to make a choice. After that meeting with the General, I remember feeling sick to my stomach. I could not breathe, and my eyes were stinging from tears because I was so angry. To recall the incident now, takes me back to a place where I felt very defeated and had negative thoughts about some sort of revenge against Jean Robb. How could I, as a Black man, retaliate against a white woman without being lynched in some way. Jean Robb was determined to get me out of the Reserves or the White House.

This was all happening around the time during the Nixon impeachment allegations. So, I was very angry because I had provided services for several of those individuals connected to the Watergate saga.

After discussing the issue with my wife, I decided that I would request a discharge from the D.C. Army Reserves in 1974. I think she was so angry that I had been so well received and respected by all that she would try to pull this stunt on me. I also think she was lucky that I was a Christian and had a family to support during this period in my life. Upon returning to work that next Monday, I kept myself composed as if nothing had happened.

Jean Robb called me into her office. She was gloating and smiling sheepishly when she stated, "Have you made a decision yet?" Jean Robb had put me in a box. She would be delighted to see me squirm or beg. My first inclination was to do something egregious, but I thought of my family that I had to continue to provide for. I informed her that I had resigned from the Reserves. Jean Robb was quite disappointed; she just knew I would make the decision to leave the White House. Her wish was not granted.

The decision to leave the Guard was the hardest one that I ever had to make. It was a false choice. I did not have to leave, but she used her position to usurp my standing in the personnel office. I could not believe that she wrote a letter to the Pentagon for the sole purpose that I would not receive the direct officer commission from the D.C. National Guard, as was being considered by the Commanding General. As a result of her fixation with trying to deny me the opportunity for advancement in both realms, I lost three years of service. The irony is that there was a white person, who was also in the D.C. Army Reserves, who never experienced any of the same things that I was subjected to. He was never pressured to make a false choice. Although I requested to see the letter that Robb wrote, the request was denied. It was implied at the time that Black people were not very trustworthy. We were not allowed to see personnel related information for fear they would let others know sensitive information on Administration officials. In essence, my high security clearance meant nothing. I was the lone ranger (the only Black person) in the office, and from that point forward, it was my job to make her life just as uncomfortable as she had made mine. Before I resigned from the Reserves, the Commanding General told me that he would hold my position, since I was developing the five-year Affirmative Action Plans for the entire DCNG and had not completed it. My ultimate decision to leave the National Guard also eliminated my eventual promotion as a Warrant Officer. That was at a higher rank than Sergeant First Class, which I held prior to resigning. Further, I often encouraged and recruited females for the Guard. I eventually received a citation for my dedication in the recruitment of women for this new initiative for the Department of the Army.

We were directed to recruit females from each of the local high schools in the D.C. area which took me to schools like Dunbar, Phelps, McKinley and others. Also, we began to recruit females with children in 1973 which was a major change for the Department of the Army. To this day, these initiatives resulted in the recruitment of many people color in the reserves of all branches of the military service. For example, the recruitment of women was up more than 30%.

Upon Jean Robb's retirement, I was notified by my former captain to return to the Guard as part of the Commanding General's Staff. I retired about four years later, spending a total of over 20 years with the Army Reserves.

To provide proper context to this story, my subsequent educational goals led me into the regulatory world of Affirmative Action. While in the Reserves, I went to night school at Roosevelt High for a few years. I really wanted to get into Howard, but I only had a 1.8 GPA. Again, I was not a good student. I enrolled in Federal City College for 4 years and also took courses at Montgomery College to complete courses toward a bachelor's in business administration.

During this same time, I found out about a program where you could get a master's degree in law studies (Clinical Law) at Antioch, a small but very well-known School of Law which served as a satellite of Antioch College in Yellow Springs, Ohio[12]. The Antioch School of Law in Washington, D.C. specialized in public advocacy. By this time, I was in my mid 30's. I would often work on my studies while working on homework with my two children after a long day of work. Both of them loved the fact that I was studying with them! My wife, Jeannette who just received a promotion to management, began traveling extensively, so it was often my job to make sure the homework was done, dinner served, and putting the kids to bed. Achieving a balance during that time was something that we had to implement and achieve to make it work. Make no mistake, while working at the White House, I went to school part-time and paid for every credit. I never received any funding for educational expenses. To this day I have no idea how I made it through. My decision to go into employment law was a conscious choice. There were many more instances where I could put my position in the personnel office to good use and initiate my microcosm of the Equal Employment Opportunity Program.

Part of my responsibilities in the personnel office was to adhere to Office of Personnel Management (OPM) reporting requirements. This meant ongoing reporting about the number(s) of people employed, nationality, etc. Jean Robb was not shy about her feelings about Affirmative Action regulations and reporting. She expressed that she was very disappointed that these regulations would affect all agencies, including the White House. She also made it hard for Jim Rogers, the second in command, and I to complete the reporting requirements on time. If I recall, she questioned everyone about why we had to comply with OPM's mandate that all federal agencies had conduct annual reporting requirements.

Originally, I looked at Affirmative Action as Affirmative "Efforts". As the only Black mid-level senior specialist there, I had access to power, which meant that I had the means to help many of my folks acquire positions through using affirmative action regulations at the White House and throughout the federal government. For more than 10 years, my strategy was to forward all employment applications from minorities and women to as many agencies as I could outside of the White House. There were times when I went behind other white staffers to pull applicants that were pitched into the bin to be discarded, I would rescue those applications and forward them to various agencies.

From my point of view, my efforts were in line with the federal guidelines expressed in Affirmative Action (AA) requirements which would ideally lead to more employment opportunities for people of color. This meant that organizations would be required to develop written action plans that involved an analysis of the workforce and related practices. In my case, I felt my efforts in employment opportunities for other blacks and females were following those principles on a much smaller scale. In the community, I mentored many of them, routinely.

Contrary to popular belief, the preponderance of the people working in the White House did not have a degree. However, this did not stop most white personnel from getting promoted or getting positions over others in choice departments.

To be clear, most of the Black personnel were in service positions irrespective of their years of experience or education, relegated to secretarial positions or messenger/courier types. You would think that after the riots during the 70's, some things would have changed, but not there.

Affirmative action was to be all about balancing the playing field. Although these measures were "implemented" as well as other hiring regulations, ultimately, they were not honored by the establishment. White folks were deliberate when making personnel decisions and supported each other openly. An example of this was when I overheard a white senior level official tell another white official that they had to give "Tom", a white individual senior level employee, a chief position because he had four kids. In essence, he was then given a promotion, not based on merit or education, but just his "social standing" despite there being several other Black candidates who were far more qualified with education and experience in finance. Tom inevitably received the GS-14 position over two highly qualified Black candidates who had also applied for same the position.

As a personnel specialist, I often questioned these decisions and was always told to back off. Many times, I would witness Black people training new white employees how to perform in technical positions or teaching white college students who had just got out of school to do their jobs. It is hard to explain how degrading it was for a Black person, educated, with a college degree, and more than capable to do the job, to train someone who does not have equitable credentials. However, this is something I witnessed time and time again during my tenure working with the federal government.

If you worked in the White House Travel Office, it was a plum position. Those people were usually GS 11's and 12's, and they were paid very well. There were about 12 white males in the department. Their role was conducting advance work for the President when he traveled. I had asked the Manager of the Travel Office on several occasions about hiring at least two African Americans. This went on for about 3 years. He would always say he would "look into it", but it never materialized. Although I had the position in personnel, it was hard to get those positions because the culture was "fixed". In other words, there were certain positions that Black folks were never going to get.

To increase the number of Black people for promotions, I started to coordinate with the Chief of Administrative Services. There were periods where the heads of different divisions would send promotions into the personnel office. I assumed that they were being advised by my supervisor when to submit them. I began to see a pattern when it came to personnel actions being taken. Most of the Black people worked in Administrative Services, so I developed a strategy. When those units recommended promotions for many of the white employees, I would write up a listing of Black employees that were eligible for promotion and submit them at the same time. I would contact George Parker or Addison Wilborn who were both Black and were supervisors of the Administrative and Miscellaneous Services Unit. This unit included drivers, couriers, and other support personnel. Before the list of promotions was submitted to our office, I would secretly request from Parker or Wilborn the list of names and put them in along with the other mass promotions at the same time. To avoid detection of my strategy, I would take the files home and sit in front of my typewriter in my basement to type up the transmittals for the persons that they identified as being eligible.

My system consisted of writing brief notes about the applicant, then, I would sign my name and funnel it to outside agencies. My transmittals were on White House stationery that I had squirreled away and brought home. The next day, I would give it a personal touch by hand-carrying them to the mailroom for delivery. The promotional actions would land on my desk from the Personnel Officer at the same time. No one would notice that all these Black folks were receiving as many promotions as possible in other positions that paid more. I slowly gained a reputation at work and on the Hill as the "Brother" in the White House.

In human resources, you routinely review and mitigate grievances of employees. Most of the Black employees would contact me when there were grievances or EEO related issues that needed to be mediated on an informal basis. There were so many more instances where I witnessed Black personnel subjected to disparate treatment than their white counterparts, but I would always try to get some type of resolution. Usually, I had to intervene due to the threat of the Black employee being reprimanded or terminated for reasons unrelated to the circumstances of their employment. This was oftentimes due to a disagreement of some sort; management was often willing to just fire them.

In one incident, a Black male who was a messenger, had a dispute with his wife the night before. For some reason the D.C. police were called to resolve the matter. The man gave the police his White House ID card which showed that he was employed there. In less than a few hours, this information was magically forwarded to someone at the White House and the next morning the Secret Service Guard took his ID and told him that he was terminated. The employee (Rob) called me for help, he had never been involved in anything like that before and had worked at the White House for more than five years. Although his termination stood, we found him another job at HUD. In another instance, another Black person got in contact with me after their badge had been taken. He advised that he and his wife had an argument over the weekend. Due to the intensity of the argument, the police were called and he showed them his ID. Again, this information was immediately conveyed to the White House secret service, and when he showed up for work the next day, they took his badge at the door. He was quite upset that he could possibly lose his job. He was a professional, had a degree, and was a documents analyst. His job was to respond to general inquiries to the President and fashion responses. He was authorized to sign the President's signature. I eventually assisted him in finding another position at another agency.

The D.C. Police were so quick to report Black personnel. It appeared there was common understanding that if you were Black then the information would be quickly dispatched to their respective managers at the White House. To be clear, this could be for any kind of conflict *outside* the realm of work. This could be any type of dispute anywhere; a store, parking lot, restaurant, anything that would involve the police, they could be terminated.

On the other hand, many whites, regardless of where they worked within the Administrations, were often given waivers and a brief admonishment by my office (by me or Jim Rogers), and "warned" that it should not happen again. White employees could be involved in several different and/or egregious actions such as driving drunk and/or charged with disorderly conduct by D.C. the Police. White personnel were often released once they would show their White House ID passes. When these instances surfaced, I would often make strategic comments, so that other white co-workers would hear what I was saying. I did this to let others see how unfair this treatment was being administered. I think the office became more sensitive in this regard. When I challenged this disparate treatment in front of my supervisor (Jean Robb), I was informed by her that this was the policy and practice of the Administration, and I should not challenge it. Apparently, we as Black people were not part of the political establishment, just mere employees. I was scolded that I needed to keep my observations to myself if I wished to remain an employee. However, this was grounds for antagonizing her further.

To have your badge taken is devastating. It happened to me over something crazy. One night I was sitting at the bar at Pier 7. I was approached by a friend of a Friend. He asked about whether I worked at the White House, which I confirmed. He started talking about President Carter having a jazz concert at the Residence. I confirmed that that was happening, but I was not going because I was going to be out of town. He ruminated about several other things; it was a casual conversation. When I returned from vacation, *my* badge was taken. The Secret Service said, "Sorry Pierpont", I was wondering what the hell was going on. I demanded to see someone. Finally, Harden Carter, who was the Chief of Staff, talked with me. He informed me that this man and his wife showed up at the jazz event, gave the Secret Service my name and stated that they were on the list. When they were told they were not on the list, he went on and on using my name and how I promised that they would be able to come to the event. Apparently, they made a big deal of it.

Due to everyone knowing me and my character, they let them in. After talking with Harden and explaining the course of events, they gave me back my badge. After that day, I went down to Pier 7 a few times a week to find the guy. I did not know his name nor affiliation with anyone I knew, but I remembered his face. Then one night, about a month later, we locked eyes, I recognized him and jumped off my seat and began to run after him.

I do not know how he got out so fast, but I was unable to find him. I never saw him again.

Employees working in the "Residence," of the White House like the waiters and butlers like Mr. Adams the character in "The Butler", were not treated fairly. The hours and the lack of empathy displayed was reminiscent of working in the "Big House". Usually, this group who served the President and others in the residence had to work six (6) days a week, often for 12 hours, and would only be compensated for five and a half days. This was in violation of the current labor laws, but no one challenged them. I was often called to see if there was something I could do, but I was constrained to do anything about it due to the nature of my job. I was often present in the middle of these disputes, and I heard several concerns such as not being properly compensated for working mandatory overtime, sometimes up to 10 to 15 hours. Through ongoing negotiations, the personnel in the residence started to receive just four hours of overtime every two weeks. Although this did not cover all those lost hours, this is what was agreed upon. To add insult to the issue, personnel were told that they would have to stop complaining when the issue was resolved. The caveat to this was that we all were Excepted Service employees. We were often reminded of the ease that folks could be shown the exit.

The examples of disparate treatment are countless, so I continued to question the practices of the hiring and promotion process. After a few run-ins, management began to make the selection process more in line with OPM regulations to avoid possible discrimination charges by other staffers. I would like to think that I played a role in ensuring that people started adhering to the guidelines to promote a degree of fairness in the selection process.

Chapter 7

Honeymoons, Cadillacs, and Foolishness

If you worked for the Administration, it was thought of as a prestigious position. I always wore my proverbial shirt and tie. Like most Black folks, I took pride in my appearance and was always raised to maintain good grooming and look presentable. Now, I had a penchant for ties, I always bought them to complement my standard suits (gray, brown, navy blue, and black). When I first started at the White House, I would get a few inquiries from white colleagues about personal aspects of my life as well as compliments on my clothing. At the beginning, I did not think much of it, but as my tenure extended, it became a daily inquiry and more intrusive... "Where did you get that tie?"...."How much did this one cost", "You are always trying to look good". Well, little did I know that these inquiries were basically "How can I afford anything on my salary". Several incidents in the office made it very clear that it just was not acceptable to be "uppity", which translates into a Black person cannot have better clothing, car, salary, or be a confident individual in the white world. In my naivete, it took me time to put these pieces of the dynamic together. It all became clear when I drove the new Cadillac to work.

It is strange how fate takes my life on roads less traveled. This happened with Ron Geisler, chief executive clerk of the White House.

Geisler headed a division of about 300 people and had worked in the White House for about 20 years. Ironically, he had this position because of the assistance I gave him. Over the years, Ron and I formed what I thought was a solid friendship. We had long conversations and often hung out together after work at the neighborhood bar. Ron advised that he was seeking a promotion and asked me for help. I helped him take a couple of correspondence courses on law as he did not have a degree. He stated that he would advocate for my transfer to the Presidential Records Office and possibly a promotion for me once everything was in place. As a favor, I wrote out the position description and gave it to him so that he could apply for an upgrade for his position. Given our alleged friendship, I believed him when he stated that he would help me. However, when the time came to make the transfer, I am pretty sure that Jean Robb blocked it. She would often say that I was too important to be moved and she would not grant me a promotion. However, there is another side to the story.

Back to the Cadillac. First, let me say, I have never been a Cadillac or flashy car kind of person. I was perfectly happy driving my Volkswagen to the ellipse and park for free every day. My wife stated she wanted a new car, that new car being a Cadillac. I must say that I did not support the purchase. I felt it was a luxury expense we did not need. We went back and forth about the car however we ended up purchasing it. I must say, it was a beautiful and classy vehicle.

Now, if you are an African American person, you probably know about a lot of the stereotypes that have been recycled for ages. When Black people demonstrated they could afford cars and homes, there were always lingering questions of the legitimacy of such purchases and the implication of doing something illegal to have the money to make those purchases.

In the 60's, 70's and 80's there was the prevalent perception that all Black folk wanted a Cadillac. This was bolstered by the fact that many African

American luminaries bought them as a sign of prestige. To throw in a little history, Black people invariably helped the Cadillac brand to become one of the longest surviving brands in the automotive field. Cadillac was introduced as General Motor's Luxury Brand in 1903 and became known for its automotive engineering, posh design and overall driving experience. However, Cadillacs were not sold to Black people, it was a company policy. Those African Americans who had a Cadillac, mostly entertainers, boxers, doctors, or realtors, would have a white friend or manager buy the car for them. However, when Cadillac sales began to nose-dive during the 1930s due to a marked decrease in affluent white customers due to a tanking economy, Cadillac reconsidered their strategy by marketing to Black customers. It was through those sales to African Americans that Cadillac averted bankruptcy. The company ended up selling enough cars to break even by 1934. [13]

Given the history and stereotypes, the last thing I wanted to do on my job was show up in a Cadillac. As fate would have it, one day when I had to go to work, my VW broke down and I had to take it to the shop...I had to drive the Cadillac to work, I was hesitant. Initially, I wanted my wife to just drop me off, but she had a scheduled appointment. So, I drove and as customary, and parked on the Ellipse. When I arrived, maybe it was my imagination, but there seemed to be more people driving in than usual. I tried to be discreet and parked it away from my usual space. As soon as I got out of the car and retrieved my briefcase, I heard Ron say, "Hey Pierpont, you got a new car?" By the time I turned around from locking the car, there were people gathering around and asking so many questions at one time. I responded to Ron and said, "this is Jeannette's car" and started the trek toward security. By the time I got to the outer offices, people were asking me about the car. I could not believe it. I mean, who needs a social media page? People get the word out when they are motivated to gossip. I found out that Ron Geisler was reporting to everybody that I had a "Caddy."

Not five minutes after sitting down at my desk, my boss came up to me and stated he heard I had a new Caddy, I looked at him with an expression of *and - so*? To me, this was all about envy and racism. I naively thought that would be the end of it, but I was wrong. Events that followed that next day, indicated that I violated the "uppity clause".[14]

Charlene, the Assistant Personnel Officer approached me and asked did my wife get a new promotion or something because she could not understand how we could purchase a new car when both our children were in private schools. I responded that it was none of her business. Within a week or so later, Ron came up to me and stated "Well, Pierpont, remember the promotion that we talked about the other day? I am so sorry, I cannot get it done for you now however, I will continue to work on it, but it does not look good." He smiled through the whole shuffle. I did not say anything and resumed my tasks for the day. I was extremely angry. In my mind, I wanted to reach over and take out every racist experience I ever had on him, but he would not have survived. To this day I have no recollection of how I got through the day as my internal rage was stoked. This incident was surely the worst during my tenure at the White House. I left the White House in 1980 during the Jimmy Carter Administration. I did not talk to Ron until about 10 years later, when I received an unexpected call from him. He stated that he was retiring from the White House, and he wanted me to come to his retirement party. When I expressed hesitance, Ron practically resorted to begging, I consented. I reasoned that it would be nice to see some of the veteran staff that I had not seen in a while, and I never turn down a decent chicken dinner. When I walked into the room, it was packed, there were over 300 people there. I engaged with several guests I knew and was on my way to another table when Geisler went to the podium and started to give his farewell speech. I leaned against one of the columns in the room while he started to talk. Midway through thanking people, he asked "Where is Pierpont?" I raised my hand, and he looked at me and began to tell the crowd what a wonderful person I was and, if it was not for me, he would not have been in the position he was in. At this point, I had little emotion about it as I had to get past the incident for my own sanity. Thinking it was over, he then said, "Pierpont, they were not ready for you. You came too early", which inferred that had I not been Black, I would have been the Deputy and taken his place as the Chief Executive when he retired. In my mind I was thinking, *what the hell*? He ruminated about it for another minute; basically, expressing his guilt in front of everybody. I lazily raised my hand and gave a slight smile; I just wanted it to stop. After his speech, I went to my car and left. While driving home, I had mixed emotions and realized I had not put the incident behind me as I began to have flashbacks about Ron standing at my desk with that rumpled blue tie. I had thoughts about how that incident with the earlier incident basically changed the course of my life.

When I came home, it was quiet. I took off my tie, went to the kitchen and looked in the refrigerator. I grabbed some cold chicken and a beer, sat at the table, and realized I was hungry. I did not eat anything at that dinner. She thought she won!

Jean Robb retired about two years after the Reserves incident. Jim Rogers replaced her. I talked to Rogers about going back to the Guard and we came to an agreement that I would return to the Guard that same year. Rogers remained in the position until the Carter transition team came in and began a major reorganization. As it turns out, the new Director of Personnel of "Office of Administration" would also give me headaches. His name was John Heist. He exercised his white privilege to the hilt. I got caught up in it, and to this very day I am still incensed.

One day John Heist ordered me to sign a promotion action for a "Sharon" who was on detail to the White House from OPM. They gave me three days to sign the promotion. I resisted by telling Ray Kogut, the newly appointed deputy, that I did not know the individual seeking the promotion. I did not like the pressure. I went to Alice Bell, a Black secretary and asked, "Who is this lady"? Alice stated she was a nice lady in a non-committal tone. I had a feeling she knew what was up, she politely excused herself from the conversation. After that both John and Ray cornered me and delivered what I perceived as a veiled threat. I had to sign it as soon as possible, before the weekend. Further, John promised me a promotion. Thinking more of my family and career than protocol, I felt I had no choice but to sign it.

The next week, I was informed by the secretary Alice, who was Black, that John and Sharon had just got married and were on their honeymoon. What? This, right after he pressured me to give her a promotion, even though she never worked for me. I waited for John to return; I was very angry that I had promoted his new wife after she returned to OPM. I didn't even know that they were dating. To add insult to injury, I found out later that she was a GS 14. In essence, I signed papers to promote someone to a higher GS grade than I was. She was now a GS15, based on my personnel action and my signature. Looking back on it, I cannot believe that I *believed* that I would get that promotion. In retrospect, they bullied me on this!

When John came back from his 2-week honeymoon, I confronted him. I stated, "John that is the worst thing that someone could do, have me sign to promote your wife". He started smiling as though he was mocking me. I stated, "if I did not have a family, I would come over there and knock you out...when am I going to get my promotion?" He stated, "we are working on it". To make matters worse, when I got back to my office after the confrontation, the support staff told me that Ray, was taking over my office. Ray was now the new Deputy Director of personnel, and I would be moving to a smaller office. Ray told me to my face they knew

I was an angry Black man, and he was sorry about everything. He also told me they were doing new assignments, and I would have move out of my office because of the change. Although on detail, Ray was given the option of being permanent and he wanted my office. With the tides turned against me, I was moved into a smaller office, but it did not stop me from demanding what was due to me. I went into John's office a second time and demanded my promotion. When he stalled, I stated "someone is going to get hurt". They acted like they feared me at that point because I was so angry that I had been played and used by them.

I was deeply upset because I was made a fool to believe I would get my promotion by signing for another person to get *their* promotion, who turned out to be his new wife, Sharon. I decided I would have to look for another position immediately before I would do something radical. I wanted to file a discrimination complaint, but I had no grounds to prevail as John never put anything in writing. In short, I was betrayed and conned, once again. However, I knew they needed me because I was handling several black employee issues that had the potential to be a major class action suit within the Office of the President. Seeking WIN-WINS, I mediated several of their disputes, which resulted in changes in Black promotion opportunities, etc.

Ray, the deputy, was in on the whole promotional thing. He also suggested I find another position and leave since I was not satisfied with current arrangements in the office. During this period, I was also attending graduate school and was taking several law courses at night. I just wanted to just get out of there because I was the only one being harassed and discriminated against. I left six months later and would eventually file a discrimination suit two years later. It was a total mess.

However, during this time period, several black employees from OA-OMB had approached me concerning the lack promotion opportunities, etc.

Their issues were that white male employees were often receiving promotion as soon as they were eligible but, similar situated professional blacks had to wait until budget restrictions were lifted months later, etc. They were not satisfied with this, so they began to file formal complaints based on race and sex discrimination against OA. At that time, the development of the Black Caucus was in play for the sole purpose of assisting other blacks that were being subjected to this form of discrimination. John was aware that I had been notified by the black employees and I was counseling them and trying to address these complaints, informally. Through my intervention, several of them received their promotions and other satisfactions. The black employees realized that management was not treating them fairly, so many of them joined groups like Blacks in Government (BIG), NAACP and the Urban League to get some outside support. This was done because many of the employees were aware that I had been selected for another position at the Department of the Interior, Bureau of Mines and the Office did not have anyone else to help them.

Chapter 8

Pictures of The Past

Wedding
1968

Pierpont's Surprise Birthday Party
2019

President Lyndon Johnson & Lady Bird
Wedding Present

Pierpont & Jeannette
50th Anniversary

Promoting Black Men Voting
Photo Credit: TMO Photography

Christmas 2022
with Children & Grandchildren

Graduation from Law School
with Mother Geneva, Jeannette & Patricia

Christmas 2022
with Children & Grandchildren

A Family Photo
with Jeannette, Tony & Patricia

Pierpont & Jeannette Receiving
Presidential Lifetime Achievement
Award 2022

Family Outing
with Children & Grandchildren

Pierpont at holding WH plaque
showing 4 Presidents when he left
Photo credit: TMO Photography

Mother-in-Law Lois Marshall Hayes & Mother Geneva Lott Mobley
Family Influencers

Pierpont Back at White House
2024

Pierpont
with his Brother Clarence

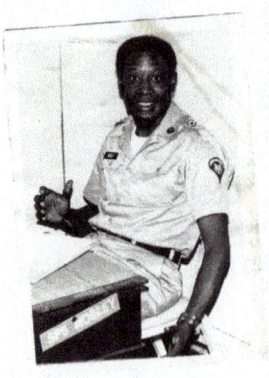

DC Military Reserves

Picture on Cover

Transition
Between Ford & Carter

WH Honored
with Plaque upon leaving
(shows 4 Presidents)

Gift WH Seal

Gift Presidential Cufflinks & Pins

Ninety-ninth Congress of the United States of America

AT THE SECOND SESSION

Begun and held at the City of Washington on Tuesday, the twenty-first day of January, one thousand nine hundred and eighty-six

Joint Resolution

To provide for the designation of the month of February, 1986, as "National Black (Afro-American) History Month".

Whereas in 1926 Dr. Carter Godwin Woodson launched the celebration of Negro History Week;

Whereas this observance evolved into a month-long celebration in 1976;

Whereas February 1, 1986, will mark the beginning of the sixtieth annual public and private salute to Black History;

Whereas the observance of Black (Afro-American) History Month provides opportunities for our Nation's public schools, institutions of higher learning, and the public to gain a deeper understanding and knowledge of the many contributions of Black Americans to our country and the world: Now, therefore, be it

Resolved by the Senate and House of Representatives of the United States of America in Congress assembled, That the month of February, 1986, is designated as "National Black (Afro-American) History Month", and the President of the United States is authorized and requested to issue a proclamation calling upon the people of the United States to observe that month with appropriate ceremonies and activities to salute all that Black Americans have done to help build our country.

Speaker of the House of Representatives.

~~*Vice President of the United States and*~~ *President of the Senate, pro Tempore*

APPROVED

FEB 1 1 1986

Joint Resolution
Established Black History Month

Barack & Michelle Obama

Pierpoint M. Mobley
3725 17th St NE
Washington DC 20018

Dear Pierpoint Mobley,

The victory we achieved on November 4 means so much to so many -- but to all of us, it is a stirring affirmation of our country's most fundamental promise: America is a place where anything -- anything we choose to dream together, anything for which we choose to work together -- is possible.

Ours was never the likeliest campaign for the presidency. We didn't start with much money or many endorsements. Our campaign was not hatched in the halls of Washington -- it was built by working men and women, students and retirees who dug into what little savings they had to give five dollars and ten dollars and twenty dollars to this cause.

It grew from the millions of Americans who volunteered, and organized, and proved that more than two centuries later, a government of the people, by the people and for the people has not perished from the Earth.

Pierpoint, this is your victory. But even as we celebrate, we know the challenges are the greatest of our lifetime -- two wars, a planet in peril, the worst financial crisis in a century. The road ahead will be long. Our climb will be steep. And we will be asking you to join in the work of remaking this nation the only way it's been done in America for 221 years -- block by block, brick by brick, calloused hand by calloused hand. What began 21 months ago in the depth of winter must not end on a night in autumn. This victory alone is not the change we seek -- it is only the chance for us to make that change.

Pierpoint, this is our moment. This is our time -- to put our people back to work and open doors of opportunity for our kids; to restore prosperity and promote the cause of peace; to reclaim the American Dream and reaffirm that fundamental truth -- that out of many, we are one; that while we breathe, we hope, and where we are met with cynicism, and doubt, and those who tell us that we can't, we will respond with that timeless creed that sums up the spirit of a people: Yes We Can.

For now, please accept our deepest thanks. We will never forget you.

Sincerely,

Barack Obama   Michelle Obama

Obama for America • PO Box 802798 • Chicago, IL 60680

Paid for by Obama for America

Letter Received From
Barack & Michelle Obama

Women's Equality Day, 1989

By the President of the United States of America

A Proclamation

On August 26, 1989, we will commemorate the 69th anniversary of the ratification of the 19th Amendment to the Constitution. The adoption of that amendment secured for women an equal voice in our representative system by guaranteeing their right to vote. Its ratification in 1920 marked a watershed in American history by ensuring that women, equally with men, could enjoy fully the rights and responsibilities of citizenship.

The active role of women during World War I was one important factor in gathering the force of public opinion behind the women's suffrage movement. Women already had the vote in some States, but during the war, as they became essential workers in many industries, women gained increasing voice and stature throughout the country. Thus, after years of hard work and persistent lobbying by women's rights groups, the Congress passed the 19th Amendment in June 1919. It was finally ratified by the Tennessee legislature on August 18, 1920, and proclaimed as part of our Constitution on August 26.

By securing for women the right to vote—and allowing them full participation in the political life of our country—the 19th Amendment affirmed the principles upon which our Nation was founded. In essence, it called us to remain faithful to the vision of our Founders, who had pledged their lives and fortunes to defending the belief "that all men are created equal, that they are endowed by their Creator with certain unalienable Rights, that among these are Life, Liberty, and the pursuit of Happiness." The ratification of the 19th Amendment was a poignant reminder that the civil and political rights enshrined in our Constitution are the birthright of all.

By recognizing previously disenfranchised members of our society, the 19th Amendment took a place among other great landmarks in American history, such as President Lincoln's Emancipation Proclamation and the 13th, 14th, and 15th Amendments. These legal milestones, and others that have since followed, such as the 1964 Civil Rights Act, have marked our Nation's progress in ensuring that all members of our society have the opportunity to reach their full potential.

In recent years, women have continued their remarkable achievements in virtually every field of endeavor, gaining positions of leadership in government, education, business, medicine, and the arts. During our Nation's record peacetime economic expansion these past 80 months, 53 percent of the increase in employment has been among women; the wage gap has been closing; and today, increasing numbers of women are obtaining undergraduate and professional degrees.

On this 69th anniversary of the 19th Amendment, it is appropriate that we recognize the many accomplishments of women, as well as their unique role in keeping our families, communities, and Nation strong. But today let us also renew our commitment to protecting the rights of all Americans, so that the United States might truly be a land of "liberty and justice for all."

NOW, THEREFORE, I, GEORGE BUSH, President of the United States of America, by virtue of the authority vested in me by the Constitution and laws of the United States, do hereby proclaim August 26, 1989, as Women's Equality Day—a day to commemorate the 69th anniversary of the ratification of the 19th Amendment. I call upon all Americans to observe this day with appropriate programs, ceremonies, and activities.

IN WITNESS WHEREOF, I have hereunto set my hand this fifteenth day of August, in the year of our Lord nineteen hundred and eighty-nine, and of the Independence of the United States of America the two hundred and fourteenth.

[signature: George Bush]

National Women Equality
Day Established

Early WH Days with Admin Staff
(Pierpont standing on right side)

President Ford Surprised visit
with co-worker Lou Ann Francis looking on

LBJ with Administrative Staff
Early Days (Pierpont last row on left)

President & Mrs. Gerald Ford
Expressing Appreciation for his Service

DC Hall of Fame Walk, all 20 class years
9th & K St, NW across from the DC
Convention Center on grounds old
Carnegie Library

2020 Induction into the Washington
DC Hall of Fame Society, Inc.

Surviving the Pandemic
Photo Credit: TMO Photography

Amias, born March 2024
Blessed to have our 1st grandson

MY ATTITUDE

I Promise Myself--

To be so strong that nothing can disturb my peace of mind.

To talk health, happiness and prosperity to every person I meet.

To make all my friends feel that there is something in them.

To look at the sunny side of everything and make my optimism come true.

To think only of the best, to work only for the best and expect only the best.

To be just as enthusiastic about the success of others as I am about my own.

To forget the mistakes of the past and press on to the greater achievements of the future.

To wear a cheerful countenance at all times and give every living creature I meet a smile.

To give so much time to the improvement of myself that I have no time to criticize others.

To be too large for worry, too noble for anger, too strong for fear, and too happy to permit the presence of trouble.

MY ATTITUDE...IS MY LIFE!

Chapter 9

Presidential Report Cards, Republicans, Democrats

The White House had the kind of culture that you did not really find in any other government agency. All the positions were very political. I served under four Administrations, two Democrats (LBJ and Jimmy Carter), and two Republicans (Nixon and Ford). Each Administration had a type of personality and with that came the staff that often mirrored the specific style of leadership.

Many people are not aware that the White House always had a permanent staff that remains to assist new Administration members and provide continuity to the protocols of the Offices. Back in the 70's the staff consisted of at least 30 employees in Central Files, 25 in the Correspondence Office, 5 in Supplies, 6 in Press Release, 8 in the Presidential Records Office, 12 in the Administrative Office, 10 in the Transportation Office, 4 in the Chief Executive Office, and 9 in the Personnel Office. In addition, there was a staff of employees assigned to the Situation Room along with 15 in the Messenger and Miscellaneous Office, and about 5 in the Press Office. Most of these individuals were on detail from other agencies. Some would be on detail for more than 8 years before they were picked up by the White House. The First Ladies' Office had about 5 employees, which was separate from the West Wing, the Main Office, which was in the East Wing.

The White House had a limited budget so there was a small group of employees with permanent status. In addition, there were many military personnel in a variety of positions such as the Navy Mess, butlers, grounds people and waiters who were paid by the Department of the Interior and the Navy Department. There was also the Vice President's Office, which was separated from the main Office in the Old Executive Office Building and a White House Communications Office, which was generally run by members of the military.

I worked in the White House through 3 different Administrations and over two/thirds of Carter's. The following are my experiences and impressions of each.

Chapter 10

LBJ

In November of 1963 when Kennedy was assassinated, LBJ was sworn into office 2 hours after Kennedy's death. It is interesting to note that this event in History led to a constitutional change, the 25th Amendment. Technically, the Constitution never spelled out how a Vice President would become President if a President died, resigned or was unable to perform the office's duty.[15]

The era of LBJ was interesting. He was well respected during his Administration. Social justice issues were at the forefront and the Civil Rights movement was in full swing. Johnson was a savvy politician, and he responded to the pressure from the leaders of the movement by signing into law the Civil Rights Act of 1964. This was the most comprehensive civil rights legislation passed by Congress since the post-Civil War Reconstruction era. The Act outlawed racial discrimination in employment, education and housing; barred racial segregation in all state-sponsored public places (such as schools, buses, parks and swimming pools) and outlawed discrimination based on race, color, religion or national origin in hotels, motels, restaurants, theaters, and all other public accommodations engaged in interstate commerce, exempting only private clubs, without defining "private." The Civil Rights legislation laid the groundwork for the Voting Rights Act of 1965, which set rules to protect the right of African Americans to vote. This act had been curbed in the states of the Confederacy since the end of Reconstruction. LBJ used about 80 monogrammed pens to sign the bill, which he gave away as mementos of the historic event. One of the first pens went to Martin Luther King Jr. who would be assassinated 4 years later. [16]

During the Johnson Administration, things were run according to protocol. The staff that came on board respected our respective positions, and we all worked well together. In fact, support staff in the Mansion were welcoming and very respectful to the entire staff. Many would invite us for free drinks while the President was in the Residence for the evening. After major dinners, we would often take food home. It was a different culture than the Nixon Administration.

One of the incidents that stands out for me during this time was an interaction with Vice President Hubert Humphrey (HHH). I was sitting at my desk and when I went to get up - I could not walk, my legs did not work, I was paralyzed. Jean Robb called the Naval Medical Unit, and it was requested that I be seen as soon as possible.

They wheeled me to the medical unit to be seen by LBJ's personal physician, Dr. Tekash. I was laying on the gurney, and up walks Vice President Hubert Humphrey. He had come to the medical unit for his annual physical. He asked what the problem was, and the physician advised him of the issue of my paralysis. In deference to the VP, Dr. Tekash, said that he would conduct the examination. However, Humphrey insisted that they continue to work with me and he would reschedule his appointment for a later time. I thanked him for his consideration and admired the fact that he showed empathy for my situation.

As I recall around one month later, his staff gave me one of his HHH lapel pens and wished me well when I returned from being on sick leave. He was a genuinely nice and thoughtful individual. LBJ's Administration was highly respected by the support staffers and they encouraged positive teamwork throughout the Office.

Chapter 11

Nixon

The level of camaraderie and working together went right out the window during the Nixon era, the entire atmosphere changed. They appeared to be superia-types.

Throughout Nixon's tenure as a Republican, he tried to "undo" some of the legislation that LBJ had passed. For example, Nixon hired several Black men to promote legislative changes and defend his actions because certain provisions in the Civil Rights Act should be eliminated or modified (such as voting rights).

Nixon did all of this to appease the Republican party, but also to appease his perspective on his own racist views. It is documented in the archives that Nixon believed in treating people according to their race, and that race implied fundamental differences in individual human beings. Nixon's racism matters because he allowed his views on race to shape U.S. policies—both foreign and domestic. His legacy needs to be viewed through that lens.[17] (See attached documents)

Nixon was not known as an outwardly friendly individual and appeared awkward in social situations. During this period, I met several of his immediate staff members during HR orientations. I interacted with many staffers who reflected Nixon's stoic personality. Many of them came across as very negative people who wanted to show how superior they were. There were a few who were generally cordial and friendly, like John Dean and Dwight Chapin. Several of the Blacks were cool also - Art Fletcher, John Wilks and John Roberts, the photographer, etc.

Although they were very professional, most of the Nixon crew were often demanding and treated the support staff as though we were underlings.

It got so bad that many Excepted Appointment employees wanted to leave within 6 months of Nixon's Administration to return to their home agencies, even though some had no choice. Consequently, this caused a lot of internal disputes. After those tumultuous 6 months, things calmed down when the new staffers realized that they had to rely on permanent staff for all types of assistance.

During this Administration, as others before, it was our job to inform personnel regarding protocols. I had to advise them of their boundaries, because they often dismissed many of the things that were emphasized and cited during orientation. My responsibilities included orienting staffers on the Hatch Act and other types of federal personnel regulations as well as employee relations (i.e., mediating disputes, etc.) I also managed the consultancy program, which involved dealing with many top administrative officials who were allowed to not be visible on the rolls. I think this was because of security reasons. Many of the consultants tried to get over with their time and attendance by adding additional hours. Most were paid $100 per day, which was great money back in the 70's. I am sure they were not happy that I, a Black man, was responsible for managing their consultant payments. When I had to make changes to their individual bi-weekly invoices, due to erroneous claims such as additional hours on their time sheets or turning them in late, it was frequently an argument, but I always held my ground.

The most impressive event during the Nixon era was during the Watergate era. During the infamous hearings, the Administration was in flux. There was a lot of talk around the water cooler debating whether Nixon was on the verge of being impeached. Most of the permanent employees, like me, stayed out of everything.

In the epicenter of Watergate, the White House staffers were constantly changing. The mood was uneasy and angry, no one trusted anyone during this period. To be in control, staffers consistently questioned why things were done a certain way and wanted to change protocols that had been in place for ages.

The environment was very toxic. Many were afraid that they were going to be fired for just small things like being late for a meeting or discussing their job responsibilities with others outside of the White House.

Throughout the 10-month period of the impeachment proceedings the entire Personnel Office was often warned not to discuss any aspects of the Nixon- Watergate situation. As a senior personnel specialist, I was selected to provide various FOIA requests[18] from the media and Capitol Hill concerning elements of the break in. This often led to disputes with my boss, personnel and administrative officials regarding what information we could release to the media, government officials, and others. Since many journalists in the White House Press Office knew I was involved in most employment matters, I was often questioned whether I had any details about the actual break-in. In addition, there were always questions about the consultants that were paid handsomely for their time, and whether these consultants were being paid from the coffers of the white house.

I was constantly instructed not to give out information that would compromise the sanctity of the White House, which limited the type of information I could send. For example, I could not reveal whether anyone who may have been involved in the break-in was on the WH payroll at the time. This period was very stressful for me as I did not want to lose my job. Further, I was enrolled in college and was taking several law classes during the evening, so I was very careful not to put myself in a compromising situation.

As far as Congress was concerned, I had to produce the documentation. However, the policy was highly scrutinized. Every organization wanted to know what role the personnel office played during this entire matter. This was a very taxing period for me because the personnel office had to provide information on personnel actions and other documents that were requested by Congress and news media in this regard. Again, I was the primary personnel specialist responsible for those consultants that were mentioned during the Watergate proceedings. However, none of this was revealed during the investigation. People often ask me what I knew about Watergate. I never knew anything of substance, because management kept our office in complete "lockdown". I was constantly warned not to discuss things with anyone and keep everything confidential. However, several news media tried, but I avoided them.

On a lighter note, during this time I was able to connect with several prominent Black officials who worked in the Nixon Administration. One was Arthur Fletcher, known as the grandfather of Affirmative Action. Arthur (Art) Fletcher had served as Assistant Secretary of Labor under the Nixon Administration, Staff Assistant at the White House. We became friends and he imparted great wisdom on me while we were trying to debate on how to roll out Affirmative Action regulations for the federal, state, and private sectors. Art was vested in the idea of Affirmative Action to help mitigate issues for upward mobility for people of color as well as women in the workforce. He was highly respected in the Administration, and along with several others, and was truly dedicated toward equal employment opportunity.

"He would often say to me and others something like, Affirmative Action ensures that the pool of qualified applicants for jobs, schools, and contracts is diverse, and includes people of all backgrounds"

I also had the opportunity to interact with other black officials there such as John Cowherd, Bob Brown and Stanley Scott, just to name a few Black Republicans. They would occasionally question me about why I was a Democrat. They believed that it was all about Economics, and as a Democrat, I would never be financially secure. It seemed as if their focus was always about money and not necessarily helping others. This impression stayed with me because I felt they (Black Republicans) were not interested in leveling the playing field to help other blacks obtain success in the world of work. It seems they were not interested in that.

Chapter 12

Ford

Personally, I was happy when Nixon resigned. All the inquiries during Watergate and walking the fine line with the press took a toll on my mind and my health. It goes without saying that the frenetic activity in the personnel office died down during the Ford Administration. Things were calmer and easier going as most of the staff had government experience. Many of the Nixon crew left and a decent batch of staffers came in with Ford. Support staffers were treated with more respect than in the past five years with Nixon. Many of the senior staff remained, which meant no major disruptions with the transition. The only highlight of the Ford Administration was the action to pardon Nixon. During that period, our office received many calls from the media. What Ford was not known for is his record on Civil Rights legislation. During Ford's tenure in Congress and during the presidency, Ford consistently supported Congressional civil rights efforts. He voted in favor of guaranteeing voting rights for minorities by twice opposing the poll tax (1949, 1962), opposing literacy tests for those with a sixth-grade education (1963), supporting court-appointed referees to guarantee voting rights (1960) and favoring additional enforcement powers against those trying to deprive others of their voting rights (1956,1957, 1963, 1964). He repeatedly supported efforts to provide federal assistance to aid in school desegregation efforts (1956, 1963, 1964) and consistently favored the establishment, continuance and broadening of the Commission on Civil Rights (1956,

1957,1963, 1964). Later he voted for the 1964 Civil Rights Act which covered voting rights, discrimination in public accommodations and facilities, and school desegregation. During this period, he also supported equal employment rights and opportunities in the form of a voluntary Fair Employment Practices Commission (1950, 1963) and equal pay for equal work by women (1963).[19]

Chapter 13

Carter

When President Carter won the election over Ford, I was reassigned to the Office of Administration (OA). This change affected my direct responsibilities to both the White House and the Executive Offices of the President (EOP). In this position I was more involved with all agencies under the umbrella of the White House and EOP. Even though this broadened my responsibilities, I welcomed the challenge. Jimmy Carter was elected in 1976. He was portrayed as a humble peanut farmer from the South. This was somewhat impressive because no politician from the Deep South had been elected to the Presidency since 1844.

Carter was the son of a preacher and routinely had Bible study in the White House. Carter was born in the segregated, southwest Georgia town of Plains in 1924, but he was raised in the nearby predominantly Black area of Archery. What is not well known about his political course is that he lost his first governor's race because he wasn't a segregationist.[20] He was viewed by many as being a good Christian man.

Despite Carter's Dixie roots, the incoming president boasted a large Black fan base, having supported Black causes as a lawmaker in his home state. Four out of every five Black voters backed Carter. His record on civil and human rights before and after entering the White House earned him ongoing support from communities of color. Carter believed in inclusion and was serious about implementing Affirmative Action efforts throughout the government.

During Carter's tenure, it was a positive working environment compared to the toxicity of the Nixon and Ford Administrations. Carter was known for bringing in the most Black and Latino women appointees out of all the presidents. This type of diversity had not been seen in previous Administrations. Many of the staff came from the Atlanta area and other Cities. Raymone Bain, Edna Draper, Robert Cotton, Valerie Pinson, Ed Maddox, Carol Jones, and Larry Bailey, all of whom invariably made major contributions during their time at the White House. Many of the new staff had never worked for the Feds. They were however willing to learn the protocols such as the Hatch Act and other important federal regulations as many of them had never served in the federal government before.

Carter made the determination that every department/agency that had over 100 employees would require a reporting requirement for the Equal Employment programs throughout the Federal government. Ruby Fields from DOD contacted me during this time. It was through her advocacy that I was able to make some changes at the White House for promotions, etc., by adhering to the regulations of the Civil Service Reform Act of 1978.[21] In this regard, I became more proactive. The Act provided guidelines for government agencies to have an Affirmative Action plan filed with the EEOC. Although the White House decided that they did not want a plan, Jimmy Carter challenged the resistance to change. Carter insisted that the White House was not exempt from these regulations, the same as other agencies. Like Carter, I asserted in stakeholder meetings that there should be a plan. I got with the Communications staff about who was employed and other demographic information. We used that information to develop an Affirmative Action Plan for the White House and the other agencies under the EOP.

There were about 450 personnel in the White House that were covered under the Executive Offices of President (EOP) workforce plan.   At the beginning of Carter's Administration major problems surfaced based on racial discrimination within the Executive Offices of the President (EOP).   The EOP included the Office of Management and Budget (OMB), National Security Council, Office of Economic Advisors and approximately six more independent agencies.   There were complaints that more Blacks deserved to be promoted during the first year of the Carter Administration.

The Carter Administration was responsive to these requests and tended to be more receptive than previous Administrations. This openness encouraged more participation with the OMB. At that agency, several issues surfaced by Black employees that resulted in several discrimination charges being raised.   Many claimed that they were not receiving promotions as their white co-workers during the previous Administration. The blacks became more proactive. There was a certain hierarchy that had been established throughout the Administration that had been going on for years. The practice of Black OMB employees training whites to do their jobs. To become eligible for a higher classification, you had to have a certain "skill set" or white supervisors would use "official" education, as the primary barrier not to promote similarly educated Black folk.   Black personnel who had trained the white employee for a particular position were often overlooked as "not qualified", even though they had just trained the white employee on how to do the same job. This usually resulted in an EEO complaint which caused a hostile working environment for the Black employee. Many Blacks and females won these cases when they filed EEO complaints based on race and/or sex discrimination.   In my case, I was unable to advance in my position because I was often tasked with assisting white employees on how to function in their positions, more effectively. The way they (whites) took advantage of us was by routinely asking questions about doing the job in question. We saw what was going on but had no power to change the situation. I was stuck at my mid-level specialist position for four years before I left the White House. I was eager to leave the White House. Once I moved over to the Office of Administration, I saw the same pattern of being placed in a similar situation. Over the course of four years, I requested a promotion three times.

Despite my range of responsibilities of managing the entire consultant program, and coordinating most ADP and personnel/payroll activities, I continued to be denied. On one occasion I was told that they had to wait until the budget was completed the following year! I firmly believe they took this stance because I had begun to work closely with the black advocacy group (The Caucus) from Office of Management of Budget and other EOP agencies. Prior to leaving, I was often assigned to attend meetings outside of the White House as a representative where many senior levels from other agencies attended. In these instances, I often resented them because I had no advanced in GS status as other attendees, mostly senior level white males. Many of the mid-level Black employees created an advocacy group to deal with complaints to top management. The main objective was to have an orchestrated way to increase promotions and remain aware of the regulations that may affect promotions.

Over the course of three years, several Black employees pressured white supervisors toward establishing a more functional employment opportunity program. This initiative resulted in more objective evaluations with the outcome being more promotions of Black employees throughout all the EOP agencies. Earlier, the issues of discrimination, lack of promotion, and harassment that transpired throughout federal agencies gave birth to forming a formal group: Blacks in Government

(BIG). BIG was incorporated in 1976 in the District of Columbia. BIG was formulated by a small group of African Americans who worked in the public health sector. Its mission was to promote equity, excellence and opportunity through advocacy, professional development, and empowerment of African Americans civil servants at the municipal, state, and federal government levels, as well as others dedicated to justice for all Americans.

BIG has since expanded and is recognized as a national non-profit organization. Ironically, BIG still engages employees in helping them to deal with the same concerns that brought the group to fruition 45 years ago. Along with the National Urban League, NAACP and other civil and human rights organizations, many Blacks and other minorities (as well as women) benefited from these organizations in promoting equal employment opportunities. These organizations were often involved in job discrimination allegations. They had a major impact on both the private and public sectors when major employment suits were raised throughout the country. Then we heard of systemic racial discord, many of us would notify the agencies' EEO Offices to get involved and openly pursue appropriate changes, which encouraged BIG training conferences.

Chapter 14

Trump

Although I had left the Feds long before Trump, he gained a place in this review due to his undoing of so many rules and regulations of the very thing that I had dedicated my life to. The Administration of Trump is the manifestation of unearthing the very foundation of *"what is fair and what is ethical?"* After training hundreds of personnel regarding diversity, inclusion, workplace harassment, career enhancement, leadership and EEO regulations, I have experienced many negative responses and challenges from specifically white males. These forums were designed to encourage positive working relations and inclusion, and to avoid conflicting situations by focusing on respecting all employees. However, these topics tended to challenge the perspective of white males. Also, some of them easily displayed "hate" attitudes often toward the career employees, which was so sad.

The Southern Poverty Law Center, which I have been a member and supporter for more than 15 years, stated that Trump appointed extremists as his key advisors at the White House and leaders within the Administration. They were devoted to rolling back civil rights protections, decimating the social safety net and implementing a nationalist worldview. Many of those in human and civil rights were so disappointed because many were such dedicated practitioners in human rights.

In 2019, I attended the funeral of a former White House staffer, Michael Sharp. His father, Grover Sharp was one of my best friends. So, I was responsible for recruiting Michael for the position in Central Files. Also, I recruited two of my nephews and many others from our communities during this period back in the 1970's. I was so proud that I was given that opportunity and all were so grateful. At Michael's funeral, I ran into several white employees at the repast who were still working at the White House after more than three decades later. They told me that the current atmosphere was the worst working environment they had ever been involved in. I personally could not believe they were still there since mid-1985.

They vowed that they were not going to retire until Trump was gone because they claimed he had shown them that he should not have ever been selected for the job of President. They also claimed that the entire Office had been so toxic that employees were not speaking to one another. "The place was nothing as it was years ago!" They talked about how they felt that no respect was given to the permanent people and that Trump's appointees looked down at everyone that was not a known Republican. Further, there were a few African American employees left at the White House but most of them resigned or retired.

They also informed me that during Trump's tenure there were very little protocols in place. It was demonstrated time and time again that they did not understand federal regulations, or anything related to political correctness. During this discussion, they expressed that this Administration failed to use the permanent staff personnel as they should have because they felt they were still working for the country and not for him. As I saw them, they claimed that they were dedicated White House employees only.

Finally, they said that there were claims from others that they were so secretive when they needed experienced staffers to assist them, they would just make their decisions without seeking assistance from them.

Meeting these former co-workers motivated me further to continue writing this book. I often felt that my experiences after leaving the White House and subsequent equal employment opportunity positions clearly motivated me toward dealing with the "Hate" issues that had surfaced more since my retirement years ago. Moreover, I definitely saw aspects of "Hate" while I was employed at both Interior and at USDA. Too often did my staff and the entire EEO community have to deal with discrimination allegations against blacks and females on a consistent basis. As I was told before I took the senior management position there, many folks called the agency; *"the Last Plantation."* There were reasons the agency had this name many years before I got there in 1989. There were long standing allegations that the black farmers were often discriminated against being denied from getting needed loans for their farms and from serving on county committees, etc. Many employees were constantly complaining about being subjected to a host of mistreatment actions based on their race and sex throughout the agency.

It had a reputation for not being willing to informally resolve these types of disputes. Employment complaints were being filed more often, which also caused very toxic and hostile working environments throughout the country. At one time, it was said that USDA had more than 120,000 employees and contractors. My unit was involved in many EEO cases there. My team and I were involved in the black farmer's class action suit that was filed around 1994.

Many of the actions taken by the white managers were often blatant acts of discrimination in the workplace before I arrived there. It seemed that many EEO complaints filed against white male supervisors were almost routine, which inferred that they were not interested in the diversity training that we were mandated to do. The training was promoted in an effort for officials to understand the EEO process as well as ways to avoid employees from feeling that they were victims of discrimination, etc. In addition, it was done so that supervisors were aware of the amendment of Title VII by the EEO Act of 1972. Title V established legal requirements for specifically, all Federal agencies to carry out affirmative employment programs under Executive Order11478. Similarly, Title VII of the Civil Service Reform Act of 1978 also required that:

The nation's workforce is reflective of the diversity of the nation as a whole.

These statues covered Federal employees only. USDA's Best Practices of Private Sector Employers falls in line with similar rules under the Equal Employment Opportunity Commission and some state human rights offices. Most of my colleagues feel as a result of these laws and regulations they forced and encouraged the diversity and inclusion movement in the workplace. Throughout my career, we took power that others had over us and create a more-fairer playing field for employment opportunities that included more diversity sensitivities.

Therefore, in today's working environment, the" replacement theories" have no place in realities. As I often stated, we should have always been respected and accepted based on our abilities and work performance.

Chapter 15

Hate Syndrome

My experience told me years ago that when I had to approach a white manager or supervisor about a discrimination allegation, he or she would automatically claim that they had not discriminated against anyone. Generally, I and members of my staff would report back that many of the involved individuals would show some symbolism of "hate" in their attitudes. However, many of my folks had been trained in conflict resolution techniques that often times eliminated hostilities during the process. Moreover, this did not stop the "Hate" attitudes by white supervisors. Many of them would begin to retaliate against those that felt they had been discriminated against in various ways, but this made it easier to seek resolutions from key management officials when they occurred.

In today's environment, one can easily see and hear of instances where "Hate" has raised its ugly head when individuals raise concerns about their rights being violated at work and also in the media, etc. As a result, this hate stuff has been on the rise since many females and black employees have raised concerns about their employment rights in both the public and private sectors.

Again, since the Civil Service Reform Act of 1978 and the establishment of EEOC years prior to this Act, many white managers and supervisors in the federal sectors seem to not worry about equal employment or affirmative employment initiatives. Again, as being one of those EEO facilitators, I still feel these acts have caused or have created sensitivities and a more effective, positive and inclusive workplace.

After taking the buy-out and retiring, my wife and I created the JPM Group, LLC, which was a management consulting firm in the mid-1990's. Our firm provided employee and management training to thousands of private and public sectors employees. In addition, since retiring, the firm has investigated and settled many human rights disputes at the informal and mitigation stages. Moreover, our consultancy firm also included a cadre of individuals with many years of human rights experience. They have also assisted clients in all aspects pertaining to Title VII of the Civil Rights Act of 1964 and EEOC. As a long time equal employment opportunity professional with a graduate degree in employment law, the firm has dedicated individuals that dealt with a host of issues pertaining to diversity. For more than four decades, I have seen many forms of hateful attitudes when I have been involved in mediating human rights disagreements. Many of us in human rights easily saw "Hate" when President Obama became President on his first day. Prior to that time, we had provided sensitivity training in the workplace for more than 20 years. However, we were disappointed that Obama's cabinet did not reflect more diversity than we had hoped originally. It seems that he chose to select not many people of color for his Administration.

However, in today's environment, The Southern Poverty Law Center asserts that there are three-point strategies to fight hate extremism.

They are, 1) Expose potentially violent extremists. 2) Fight hate in the courts and 3) Provide free training in law enforcement that will encourage our younger individuals on how to appropriately prepare to deal with them.

We were very active in the D.C. Democratic Party prior to his election. In fact, my wife and I had been leaders in at least four of the D.C. mayoral campaigns and had received the D.C. Hall of Fame Award during the past 20 years for our dedicated service to our community. In fact, my wife was a D.C. delegate when Obama was nominated in Denver. We both were there at that momentous occasion; the first black President nominee. In this instance, I was overwhelmed because I had written the first Affirmative Action Plans for the White House. I was the only black in Personnel in 1978 and had worked so hard along with wife politically to support his campaign. His nomination made us and most of our friends so proud of that moment. In fact, I cried! However, I recall my Director indicated that she claimed that the White House should be exempt from this federal ruling for all federal agencies. I began working on it and before she was apprised that it had been completed and sent to OPM. She was too late to stop the only one that was officially published. It was obvious she was not a supporter of Equal Employment Opportunity for the White House Office or the EOP.

Beyond the White House

Chapter 17

Department of the Interior, Bureau of Mines

After I left the White House, I transferred to the United States Bureau of Mines[22], (USBM) in the Department of the Interior, in 1980. I was selected as an EEO Manager, Program Planning and Adjudication Division by Ron Shelton, EEO Officer. Rick Harrison, a former friend from the DC National Guards, and Deputy Chief of Personnel, recommended me for the position because I had assisted him in acquiring his current position several years prior.

In fact, after applying for several other vacancies, Rick told me that he remembered my background and expertise in EEO and knew that I was highly qualified for the vacancy. Several days later, I was offered the position.

The Bureau was a different landscape than the White House. I noticed that most positions there were *competitively* announced, where at the White House many of the positions were political. Many people of color were promoted to mid-level positions, and many were highly educated. This was a little different from the White House as many staff members there spent many years in the same position with very little opportunities for advancement.

While at the Bureau, I continued my education at Antioch. In my 2nd year, I assisted other colleagues to enroll in the same graduate program, so that they could also receive their Master of Law Studies (MLS). This training helped to bolster our work for EEO investigations and mediating civil and human rights cases.

The graduate program also helped me with my participation in Blacks in Government (BIG) and other human rights organizations, like NAACP and the NUL. I worked toward training others in employment law in order for them to be more effective in understanding equal employment opportunity program objectives.

Back then, I recall at least three Chiefs of Research Centers displaying hateful behaviors when they were cited for being involved in the EEO discrimination complaints process. While I served as Chief of EEO Adjudications for the Bureau of Mines, I often saw how Blacks and females were subjected to forms of disparate treatment. These cases were claims by employees in Minnesota, West Virginia and in Arizona. Even though the disputes were resolved informally, they let me know that they were not sensitive toward equal employment opportunity rights. In one instant, hate was the cause that an employee jumped out of the window on the 12th floor at Columbia Plaza. In another situation, a black female was promoted retroactively for two years, after a finding of discrimination in New Jersey. She was passed over three times for a promotion by her white supervisor.

BIG and other organizations focused on discrimination issues and providing advocacy for thousands of employees shortly after being incorporated. Members would routinely lobby on Capitol Hill which increased their visibility. It was also during this time that Eleanor Holmes Norton, who was in the middle of all this, eventually became the head of the EEOC. She was one of the best there to seek justice for all. As a result of her appointment, many of us in EEO began to be more proactive in forcing agencies and public sector companies to develop more Upward Mobility Programs. These programs more training opportunities at our annual conferences so they could qualify and apply for higher level vacancies. The training motivated many of the participants at these diversity awareness conferences, both males and females.

BIG filed and won several major lawsuits throughout the government and large companies, such as the telecommunication sector and local entities. As I recall, they utilized the Civil Service Reform Act of 1978 as a foundation for changing the way African Americans were treated at the federal, state, local levels, which provided some of the protections that many people of color have today.

However, for federal employees, it was my experience that white managers were forced to accept EEO issues because it was the right thing to do.

As I stated earlier, I was eager to leave the White House so in late 1979, I was offered the position of Equal Opportunity Manager at the US Department of the Interior. As the EEO Manager in charge of Program Planning, and Adjudication at Interior's Bureau of Mines (BOM), it was refreshing to witness a positive working team environment. The position gave me a full range of responsibilities to facilitate a sound and sincere approach to equal employment opportunity for the agency. The staff were dedicated to ensuring that EEO regulations were followed. We also provided diversity (EEO) related training and onsite affirmative employment reviews throughout the many research centers nationwide. There were often racial and sexual allegations that rose but resolved.

The irony of being in this line of work is sometimes you must do the very thing that you instruct other people to do. Due to the discrimination that I experienced on my own job, I had to file a few complaints of my own. The first one, I received a call from Carolyn, one of the secretaries at the Merit Systems Protection Board (MSPB), who informed me that there was a position open for an EEO Director there. Even though I was employed at the Bureau of Mines, this position came with a higher classification level and salary than the one I was in at that time. She stated I should apply quickly since this position was a perfect fit for me, and they needed a black individual in the job since blacks were not treated fairly within the agency. As the secretary, she claimed that I had all the necessary background and credentials. She also told me that management was trying to give the position to a white female, who was not qualified for the position. I went in for the interview, was able to answer all the questions, and felt I did a great job during the interview. However, the panel did not seem to be positive about the newly created position that I was applying for. It was a secret vacancy!

Since I had worked with Carolyn before, there was really nothing they could ask me that I could not answer. It was a faster interview. I felt very positive during the interview, however, I had suspicions I would not be selected. She had expressed concern about the agency not hiring blacks for senior level positions in the past. Later, I was told by the same secretary who advised me to apply, that I was not chosen for the position. She further informed me that they hired a white female who barely had the minimal qualifications. This all led to me filing a discrimination complaint against them. My complaint was resolved several months later through an agreement via mediation. In the end it was settled for around $2,200 for compensatory damages but I just wanted to get it over with. Although it was not a lot of funds, I was satisfied with the agreement because it was a matter of principle.

My second filing for discrimination surfaced after being at the Bureau for more than 7 years against the Director of EEO. It turned out to be a messy "affair". The Director, who was also Black, allowed a very junior white female employee (GS-5 or 7) to investigate an onsite discrimination case in Alabama, even though she had no qualifications to conduct any investigation. This was against my recommendations, since I was Chief of the Branch. Giving her that assignment resulted in major conflicts within the Alabama Research Center and morphed into a major dispute with management in Alabama and our office in D.C. This almost caused me to lose my position.

The situation was investigated and because of my complaint, they both were suspended for several days until management reached an informal resolution to my satisfaction. Both of them were disciplined. This situation put me in a very precarious position, as I had filed a complaint against another Black man who happened to be the Director. The irony was he was the one that selected me for my position and helped me in my transition from the White House. Inevitably, the Director had to accept my dispute and not fight it. The office was acutely aware that he had engaged in sexual relations with this junior staff person on the job and others were aware of it. The fallout from that decision to send that person to Alabama took months to resolve. He placed the entire staff in a terrible position because we're supposed to be a model for human and civil rights, and here we were viewed as doing the opposite. He disrespected the entire office nationwide when this happened.

The Bureau of Mines was a great place to work because I had to work with other agencies within the Department of the Interior. Most of the human resources and EEO officials were very professional and were focused on upward mobility opportunities for minorities and females. In fact, if I can recall, the agency often held meetings toward being proactive in developing strategies to enhance employee advancement opportunities and agency-wide training.

While back in the White House and other federal agencies, many Black employees were designated to non-professional positions, such as Program Assistant, GS-301-6 or GS-7, without any promotional opportunities. With the backing of EOP, BIG and other federal organizations, upward mobility programs were developed. These programs helped to ensure black employees-and females were provided opportunities to advance through the government system which were usually capped at the GS-7 levels. Organizations like BIG were established because of the instances of discrimination throughout the federal government. In many instances, black personnel were routinely assigned to and had to accept lower GS grades, to progress into the professional series. In many instances, they were often overqualified (academically, etc.) but were willing to accept the positions just to get inside the government. Working in the government often was viewed as safe and had good benefits, including health and good pay.

This is why I often said that leaving the White House when I did, was a blessing because it gave me more opportunities to develop more professional skills, etc. Had I remained in the hostile working environment there, my opportunity to advance would have been harder to achieve. Remember, although I was a Senior HR Specialist, they did not have an employee training program for any employee. I always advocated for an informal one but was overruled because the political people would not allow funds to be used in that manner. They did not want to create a budget for it. Therefore, everyone interested in furthering their education at the White House had to pay for it themselves. In this instance, I did, and encouraged many of my co-workers to do the same. I often attended USDA Graduate School, at night, when I could.

Chapter 18

Major Career Disappointments

While in the D.C. National Guards, an HR official NCO denied me an opportunity to take a test for a direct Officer Commission. I was not told this until the vacancy was closed. He simply said that since I was working at the White House, "I was already privileged."

I was forced to resign from the D.C. National Guards for three years, because she said "I and my job were too important, so I needed to leave the reserves, ASAP" if I wanted to keep my position at the White House. She told me that since she did not hire me, she could fire me! As a Black man, I was very disappointed with her! She demanded that I resign from the Personnel Office as soon as I could. I laughed at her when I told her I resigned from the Guards instead of leaving the Office. She put a lot of pressure on me, and I am sure my race was the reason for it.

While at USDA, I was forced to retire early (took the Buy-out) because allegedly white farmers were looking for me due to my involvement into the Black Farmer's Class Action Suit. The Associate Chief and other senior level officials told me, informally, that the white farmers were looking for me. In addition, someone from the Secretary's staff put the word out that I should retire since I had more than 30 years with the Federal Government. I took these innuendoes seriously, along with the fact that I had applied for several other senior level positions within USDA and was not selected. I saw the writing on the wall, and I was scared! So, I retired. Lastly, a few years ago, while serving as a D.C. Human Rights Commissioner, my Appointment ended abruptly because my resume indicated I supported the Boys Scouts of America. Earlier in my childhood, I was a Cub and Boy's scout. However, acknowledging this, a D.C. group inferred that I was anti-diversity, etc.

Chapter 19

Clarence Thomas

While all the fallout was going on, there was another incident on the Hill peppered with impropriety: the appointment of Clarence Thomas to the Supreme Court. It was my understanding that he would often say inappropriate, sexually laden comments. At the time, Thomas was the Chairman of the Equal Employment Opportunity Commission (EEOC). During and after the hearings, several individuals in EEO informed me that many failed to give testimony due to the fear of being retaliated against, particularly by Commissioner Thomas and the Republicans. This was especially true for those who had worked for EEOC at the time of those incidents. Moreover, back in those days, we in EEO, found Clarence Thomas to be a strange man with a fragile ego, for instance. While I worked in the same building for the Bureau of Mines, I would sometimes use EEOC's library because most agencies in building had access to it. Most of the Federal employees there used the library. On one particular day, Commissioner Thomas approached me while I was reviewing case law for a class at Antioch School of Law. He asked me why I was in *his* library since all of "his" agency employees had recently moved to another location? I explained that I worked at BOM and further, that the library was a federal entity, and he did not have jurisdiction over who or when someone used it. I guess he did not like my response, and he suddenly became verbally aggressive. He began to "bully" me, stating loudly that I better leave, get out of his library and go to my own library. I think he was trying to intimidate me with his body language by standing over me while I was seated. I was only reviewing one case. His actions momentarily lead me to believe that he was ready for some type of physical altercation.

Although I did consider taking him on, the last thing in the world I wanted to do was to have witnesses see two middle-aged Black men fighting in a "federal" library. Thus, I looked at him and left. Because we all looked alike to the Commission in the 1980's, his appointment, by Republicans, was virtually a "slap in the face." Back then, Thomas did not believe in, nor did he support regulatory measures for Affirmative Action or the management of EEO complaints filed against any federal agencies. It was said that he was against anything that dealt with human or civil rights for individuals seeking redress from cases filed about race or sex discrimination. Many on his staff allegedly knew that he was not an advocate for equal treatment under the existing equal employment regulations established prior to his appointment as Chairman of EEOC. Also, many of us working in EEO expressed that his actions and record indicated that he was against all form's discrimination allegations in the workplace, and he was against all class action suits filed against private corporations/companies; this was one of the main responsibilities of the agency. His verbal record while so assigned will verify this. While he was addressing a session of the Black Caucus, allegedly the only one he attended, it was said, he stated because we all may look alike, doesn't mean we think alike! Many of us that were in EEO and civil rights felt that Commissioner Thomas was a disappointment. We must remember that he did not carry on a positive legacy, the same as the late Supreme Court Justice Thurgood Marshall. It follows that many EEO Managers and Specialists were not anxious to send EEO related cases to EEOC because of the lack of support. As I recall, myself and many senior level supervisors and employees in and outside of the EEOC were very hesitant to rule on cases that could have an adverse impact against national organizations.

This resulted in a major fallout in the momentum in deciding these cases due to possible retaliation from him Thomas and others like him. It was known throughout most agencies. It was alleged that EEOC would hold up major decisions dealing with Federal related and corporate discrimination suits. Thomas made the stand that he was against affirmative action by limiting the application in higher education. In his concurrence, Thomas compared affirmative action to "government-imposed racism".[23] In my opinion Thomas made a spectacle of himself amongst his colleagues and the Court by writing a concurrence that was 58 pages long, far longer than Chief Justice Roberts' 40-page majority opinion, which Thomas joined. It was reported that it was the first time in nearly 10 years that *any* justice had taken the exceedingly rare step of underlining a concurrence, not a dissent, by making an oral announcement from the bench.[24] In Thomas's oral announcement in the affirmative action case, he lashed out at the court's other African American Justice, Ketanji Brown Jackson, to make sure that the other Justices were aware of his position. Thomas's pronouncement was described as a full-on, sustained attack on Jackson by name, and her dissenting opinion in the University of North Carolina case. What's more, the attack was personal in a tone, strikingly different from the tone he used when rebutting Justice Sonia Sotomayor's dissenting opinion in the Harvard case. For page after page, he railed against Jackson's recitation of historical discrimination after the Civil War and well into the latter part of the 20th century. She bolstered with statistics showing enormous gaps for Blacks in inherited wealth, access to health care and ability to buy even a modest home or build a small business because of bank practices that red-lined African Americans out of getting loans. For six solid pages, he took aim at her dissent, contending that "on her view, almost all of life's outcomes may be unhesitatingly based on race. Such a view is irrational; it is an insult to individual achievement and cancerous to young minds seeking to push through barriers, rather than consign themselves to permanent victimhood".[25] Apparently, Thomas railed on and on about how Affirmative Action was an injustice to us all. I guess he forgot that he benefited from Affirmative Action when he was admitted to Yale Law School. Thomas arrived at Yale at the exact moment it created its first explicit affirmative action program. It was designed to set minority enrollment at about 10 percent of the incoming class. I remember during his Supreme Court confirmation hearing, Thomas stated that he believed he had earned his spot at Yale and hadn't received any special treatment due to his race.[26] By the way, many African Americans did not support his ascension to the Supreme Court. I remember my wife, I, and a bus load of folks went down to Yuba, VA to protest and demonstrate against his appointment. Back in the day, I felt sorry for him because no one appeared to like him. At EEOC he was labeled as very arrogant. I do not think that he really understood that the Republicans made sure that he was in charge because he was not supportive of Affirmative Action programs and class action suits of discrimination. I believe he had no idea he was being used. Based on our interaction with him throughout the years, It seems as though he was selected for the EEOC and the Court, not because of his intellectual prowess or respect. It was just because he was known to be hard on Black folks and he had no interest in civil and human rights. Lastly, I met Anita Hill years ago while we both worked in Columbia Plaza here in D.C. She was, and still is, a brave individual. Lastly, I personally believe that if the investigators interviewed his immediate staff about Anita Hill's allegation of sexual harassment, he would have never been selected for the Supreme Court. It was rumored that the Republicans were not willing to conduct a full field investigation on the matter. Mr. Thomas' office had several staffers willing to provide evidence, but they apparently were never contacted to provide their testimony, allegedly. The same tactics have been used over and over for decades, particularly by Republicans. The campaign to promote Hershel Walker just a few years ago reminded me of the same campaign push to promote Clarence Thomas to the bench.

Chapter 20

USDA

I n early 1989, I was offered a senior level position with the Soil Conservation Service at US Department of Agriculture (USDA). I accepted the position to head up their EEO Compliance and Enforcement Branch. There, I was provided with an excellent staff of full-time specialists and mediators (EEO Counselors), throughout the USA. There, I oversaw the entire (SCS) USDA Mediation Program (ADR), which handled EEO issues/complaints across the entire agency. At the time, the USDA had about 120,000 employees throughout the USA and abroad, I had never seen so many Black male professionals in the federal government.

This was mainly because we had many agricultural colleges and universities in the South. Many Blacks were hired after graduation due to their backgrounds in the agricultural sciences and their cooperative programs. In addition, as Chief of EEO, I was often called upon to work on special task forces and committees under Mike Espy, the Secretary of USDA. Several assignments had a great impact for USDA and other Federal agencies throughout the entire Federal workplace. One of the task force was to establish a federal policy for the new Sexual Orientation Program and it became policy.

Part of my job was to provide training to SCS employees and county personnel in the areas of sexual and workplace harassment and diversity awareness. Dubbed as the "Last Plantation" by many Black employees throughout the federal and state government, as well as the Black farmers, the agency was rife with a history of discrimination. The Secretary's Office had used me as a troubleshooter for several major racial disputes throughout the agency. Consequently, I gained a reputation throughout USDA in crafting resolutions.

While at SCS, I was also appointed as a USDA Cadre Instructor for the entire agency. This Certification was for the purpose of proving all aspects of organizational development (ADR) at the federal level. Therefore, we worked closely with HBCU programs to recruit more African Americans to various vacancies within the agency. In this position I provided training on diversity and conflict resolution and mediated employment disputes across the country.

While at USDA, I also had the most intense experience that catapulted me right into retirement. In many of the stories, it starts out small and ends up being something where I must make a hard decision.

It all started with a phone call from a white male employee from Alabama. When I spoke with him, he sounded fearful, angry, and upset about what he had seen in Florida at a conference. He told me many things that I thought I would never hear. The employee stated he had heard that I was an ex-military Non-Commissioned Officer and since he also was a sergeant in the military, he felt safe discussing his situation with me. Our conversation went on until almost midnight, we talked for about 5 hours. The white employee stated that his supervisor was trying to fire him for no reason. He claimed that while he was on a training assignment in Florida, he had the unfortunate experience of seeing one of his peers from the job (a female Conservationist) and the State Representative kissing near the cafeteria late one evening. To elude the situation, he tried to make himself invisible and went quickly up to his room. Upon his return to the Alabama Research Center the next week, his co-workers began to harass him about, implying that he was going to be fired. To him, that was an indication that he had been seen by his managers while in Florida. Although he claimed that he would never say anything, the incident was a conflict of interest further as she was married. His claim to me was that he would never say anything and never report what he had witnessed. After seeing what was going on, he then understood why this female often received promotions over many of their other Conservationists. He was suspended for several days. Management tried to sully his reputation, stating that he made others feel uncomfortable by discussing the Vietnam war too much and others made general complaints about his behavior. The employee felt that someone was going to kill him and/or his family. This employee then told me that he had been on assignment for the disbursement of government loans.

He then talked about how Black farmers had been victims of discrimination by the USDA for years. A week later, he called me and advised me that he was in D.C. and wanted to meet. We met at 12th and Independence Avenue, NW near my office. During the meeting, he and his son showed me several folders of documents that showed evidence of how whites had denied loans to Black farmers dating back many years. The documents in their possession presented clear and convincing evidence of more than 40 years of deliberate discrimination against blacks. I was overwhelmed examining the evidence. I could feel the emotions welling up within me as I tried not to cry. The documentation was from seven southern states regarding the systemic denial of loans. I could not believe that I was in possession of documents that verified and affirmed the Black farmer's experiences with the USDA. Many of the Black farmers had been fighting the government for years and were being constantly harassed when they would seek redress from being discriminated against. The next morning, I contacted one of my EEO officers about what was going on and made an informal inquiry into the allegations. The EEO officer informed me that this employee was an employee and appeared to be a person who was truthful and honest. We [I, the Whistleblower, and his son] took the evidence to the USDA Solicitor's Office the next morning. The Solicitor's Office is the law enforcement agency for the Department of Agriculture. Cases of note are often transferred to the Attorney General's Office of the United States. I encouraged several of my USDA colleagues to contact the Black Farmers to file a massive Class Action discrimination charge against the USDA for injustices dating back more than 50 years. Naturally, I was later called into the Associate Director's, Mr. Lewis', office.

He stated that he had received calls inquiring about me and my whereabouts. Some people were asking for my head on a platter. He stated, "The word is out, there are people in 3 or 4 states looking for you" "You did something...they want to know where you live and other information" "What have you done?" I told him what was going on. Mr. Lewis is black. Further, there were several things that began to happen at the agency during this period. I was being retaliated against by white managers through a coalition of southern farmers. After that meeting with Sherm and subsequent actions that seemed to be directed toward me, I went straight to personnel. I was scared and I realized I was in too deep. My only recourse was to retire so I took the buy-out and retired. I knew I was targeted because the suits could cost the USDA thousands of dollars in damages because of the proof of systemic discrimination. After nearly 31 years with the government, I decided to leave to start my own human rights firm. My decision to retire was reinforced with the fact that I had applied for three senior division EEO level vacancies within that 6-month period and was not chosen to fill any of them. All three positions had been filled by females, so I just felt that there was a trend that indicated that black males were not being selected for those senior level positions within USDA anymore.

After I retired from the Federal government, some of my EEO staff members had the whistleblowers and his family transferred out of Alabama for security reasons. This was great news for me. I will always remember that one of the main people responsible for sealing the outcome of the Black Farmer's settlement was a white whistleblower.

For decades the USDA discriminated against Black farmers by denying them loans, upending their livelihoods, and preventing them from building generational wealth.[27] After decades of longstanding racial discrimination in the administration of the USDA's loan programs, Congress attempted to correct historic wrongs with the passage of the American Rescue Plan Act which provided $4 billion dollars of debt relief to Black farmers and Native Americans. President Obama's Administration signed a $1.15 billion measure in 2013, to fund a settlement initially reached between the Agriculture Department and minority farmers more than a decade ago.[28]

Republicans were critics of the settlement from the beginning, claiming that the process was fraudulent. Before funds could be released, white Texas farmers sued the USDA to block disbursement of the funds, alleging that the loan forgiveness payments violate the U.S. Constitution. The court issued a preliminary injunction that temporarily halted the program, pushing many Black farmers to the brink of foreclosure.[29] However, the US Court of Appeals of the 5th Circuit recently reversed that decision in March of 2022.[30]

Chapter 21

Beyond The Feds

After retiring from the Department of Agriculture with more than 30 years of service, my wife and I established the JPM Group, LLC, Management Consultant firm in 1995. We and our group began to provide organizational development consultant services to both public and private sectors. Our services included all forms of workplace training and other related services that were often requested by our clients. In addition, we also partnered with other firms when it was necessary.

About 15 years after I retired, we won a bid to provide Diversity Awareness Training to approximately 200 Federal managers from USDA in Morgantown, West Virginia. I was advised that this training was mandatory because of the class action suit by the Black farmers against USDA. It was about 8 years earlier that I had left my post there. When I completed the training, one of the white senior managers saw me in the hall and hollered at me. I looked up at him and paused and I could not figure whether he was talking to me. All I remember is that he was a very large man who was red in the face and looked like a bull getting ready to charge. I kept my cool, but knew if he did anything, I was ready. He then came close saying they were tired of this "diversity stuff" and I needed to leave the city as soon as possible. He just did not know what would happen to me if I remained there the rest of the night. I guess he and others remembered my name from the past. My wife wanted me to turn him in, but we chose to return to D.C. that evening. Nothing had changed and it was not worth the confrontation. This occurred only 12 years ago! Therefore, the word "Diversity" was apparently hated by many white managers in the workplace years prior to this incident.

Chapter 22

Take a Picture: Past, Present & Future

We must tie in the past, present and the future, we will have to ask ourselves one question: how did we get to Trump? Obama was a first and was celebrated for both tenures of his presidency. Although we did not get everything that we, African Americans and other social folks wanted or needed, it was still a shot across the bow, so to speak. However, Obama's presidency was used to reignite the raw racial divide in this country. Based on fact less allegations by Trump, there was an investigation to determine whether Obama was born in this country. If we take a walk down "common sense lane", we all know that people must be vetted before seeking the office of the Presidency. How could he escape the FBI, CIA, Justice Department, and a cadre of others speculate that Obama was not born in the States? It flies in the face of reason, yet people believed it. This type of persuasion and vulnerability in this country can be dangerous, and it is one of the reasons we ended up with Trump.

The era of Trump harkened back to those days of the lyrics of Billie Holiday's song *"Strange Fruit"*. Every day was a media circus on what type of racist or crazy theories that Trump espoused. Think about this, what do their children think about this hate and extremist behavior for their future?

In the end, many White people and others supported it and became avid "followers". Personally, as I write this book after many years of being involved in civil and human rights, I often wondered why it seemed that the Republicans appear to be so angry. I am dating back to the mid 1960's, when I was just being introduced to the voting rights movement. They just appear to be so angry at black people. This includes both blacks and white folks! Could someone tell me why? In Trump's case, it appears that based on their comments, and what has occurred since his staff left the White House, he and his staff, left with little vision.

All the work that had been done throughout the 70's with the Civil Service Reform Act, Affirmative Action measures, regulations and laws that were to bring about some semblances of equality were basically ignored or not taken seriously. Trump's actions created a smoke screen to preserve the white male power structure in both the private and public sectors.

It appears we, as a society, have chosen to ignore the vestiges of what has been deemed as a "moral center". Just think about it, Trump had been accused of many sexual harassment charges and caught on tape, but he still was selected over Hillary to be president. On the Clarence Thomas matter, I still was around during this period, while he was the Chairman of EEOC and was still selected to serve on the Supreme Court. However, in today's environment, he has continued to show folks that he was not worthy enough to serve on the bench.

In the post-Trump era, we find ourselves back where we were in the 70's. Diversity training, diversity officers, inclusion, equity. These are similar buzz words that were used back in the 70's when I and others in similar positions were conducting training throughout different federal agencies and abroad.

When I conducted training, many organizations had to set aside funds outside of their existing operations to deal with diversity awareness initiatives, and we see the same actions going on in 2020. Back in the 70's Affirmative Action was seen by many white managers as a "no need act" and a misuse of government funds. This resistance to "change" caused many conflicts in the both the private and public workplace. Although we may not witness outward resistance toward the current push to "undo" many of the injustices that we were witness to just over the past 7 years or so, reports of hate crimes and senseless shootings of African Americans, particularly males, has gone up tenfold. I think what we are witnessing is a struggle that was brought about by years of resistance and hard work, to enact laws and regulations toward equity and parity in the workspace.

Due to the Reform Act and countless regulations, many Blacks and women have been placed in positions where they are able to utilize their power and expertise to change the landscape of labor.

This residual transition created a backlash as they (white males) began to realize that their "Power" was being eroded, simply because of the changes in society and in the workplace. It is no longer a white male dominated world where they make all the decisions, without someone questioning or challenging them. The "power" had been in their hands for so many years.

Chapter 23

Last Words

In the early winter of my years, after more than 50 years of federal service and consulting, I have learned a few things. Moreover, I feel as though those of us that were chosen to serve in civil and human rights areas, were dedicated to make a difference in equity for all and equal employment opportunity. One, the workplace is a microcosm of society; the discrimination and harassment on the job reflects how we treat each other. If you took a picture over 50 years ago, we have made some progress but not enough where there is not a need for this type of work. Discrimination still exists. The problems are widespread and are present in many venues. Two, different Administrations have demonstrated that the reforms that have been put in place do not always do what they are designed to do. Reforms must be *applied* if they are going to work. The courts often take too long to resolve the issue. Three, it has been my general experience that Black males seldom file charges at work. They tend to walk away from conflicting situations or discriminatory events, more so than females. I have been told by many that they are thinking about their *family* responsibilities before they take chances on their jobs as they do not want to take the risk of being fired. Four, it is oftentimes the victim of discrimination that must provide the burden of proof, which is often a deterrent to take cases to court. Lastly, the realization that the need for work that I have done will still be relevant and necessary long after I have left this earth.

It is my fervent belief and hope that through all the sacrifice of time, stress, and family, I helped to balance the scales of justice, along with scores of others, in our quest for what is right. I have been encouraged that even though democracy is still a focus by most men and women of color, expanding it nationwide is a worthwhile activity. It is sincerely necessary so our youths can focus on respecting other's differences. Therefore, individuals that are around my age will really have to step up to ensure value to other cultures. The white extremist has confronted us in today's environment openly. We now must address our efforts directly "in your face", something years ago we did not have the educational tools to effectively deal with it. There has been a change since then! I feel and see that many of our youths are dealing with overcoming deeply entrenched biases by calling it what it is: disparate treatment because of the color of our skin (brown, black, tan and interracially). Can they keep trying to keep us down just because they are failing to judge us on our merits?

They are clearly missing what the American ideal is all about. Shame on them because I mean every word......

Vice President Kamala Harris

My personal experiences and reflections have been highlighted in my book which shows the profound changes in American society over the past five decades, particularly in the realm of the advancement of women and in particular, women of color in politics.

Having witnessed Barack Obama's historic election as the first Black president of the United States was all I thought I would see in my lifetime.

However, God had another plan as South Carolina Congressman James Clyburn helped Joe Biden's fledgling campaign by telling him that he needed to put a black woman on the ticket as Vice President.

After her own failed campaign as President, Joe Biden selected Kamala Harris to be on the Democratic ticket with him as his VP running mate. It is without question that she was highly qualified for the position. A former District Attorney and Attorney General in California, the largest state in the union followed by becoming the second black female African American Senator in the US Congress. She indeed shattered the "glass ceiling".

They took office on January 20, 2021, as the newly elected President and Vice President of the United States.

On July 21, 2024, President Joe Biden dropped his bid for reelection after a disastrous debate against Trump and immediately endorsed Kamala Harris.

To think that once again, I lay witness to Kamala Harris, the first African American and Asian American to receive and accept the nomination of the national Democratic Party was something that I thought I would never see in my lifetime.

Kamala's campaign raised $200 million and got 170,000 volunteers in the first week of her campaign while setting record numbers of 15k or more at all her rallies. This grassroots enthusiasm has been embraced by every segment of our society. *Some pundits say this is just a honeymoon and the euphoria will soon be over. However, I believe the honeymoon will lead to a marriage that will lead to the presidency in 2025.*

Her selection of Minnesota Governor Tom Walz who has an impressive background and has no problem in letting voters know how crucial this election is followed by Kamala's own performance of sharing the fact that our freedom is at stake is a winning combination. I am confident that by the release of my book, we will call her Madame President as she gives a hopeful vision for what lies ahead for America.

And Joe Biden will go down in history as one of the most revered Presidents for his courageous, patriotic and unselfish act for putting country and democracy first by relinquishing his reelection bid.

Chapter 24

Wisdom is not Knowledge!

Long ago, prior to these workplace incidents, I found out that each of us must try to help others within our respective communities and at our workplaces. If we have empathy and care for one another, as I was raised on this up-bringing which encouraged me at an early age, to be respectful of others' situation. These traits have always been part of my behavior when dealing with people. Therefore, my Knowledge, Skills and Abilities (KSAs), have been used concurrently while employed as a full-time senior level manager for the Federal Government.

The Bottom Line

FACE IT, nobody owes you a living; what you achieve in your lifetime is directly related to what you do or fail to do.

No one chooses his parents or childhood, but you can choose your own direction.

Everyone has problems and obstacles to overcome, but that too, is relative to everyone.

Nothing is carved in stone, you can change anything in your life, if you want it badly enough.

Those who take responsibility for their actions are the real winners in life.

Winners meet life's challenges head on, knowing there are no guarantees, and give it all they've got.

Never think it's too late or too early to begin. Time plays no favorites and will pass whether you act or not.

Take Control of Your Life, dare to dream and take risks...Compete!

Believe in yourself because it's all up to YOU!

Author Unknown

Golden Rule: *"Treat others as you want to be treated."*

Chapter 25

"The Black Challenge"

We collectively know that when we have lost our family structures to the single parent environment, we lose our power due to fatherless.

The challenge now is we need to:

-Stop being a victim and live a good life focusing on respecting yourself if you do, they will respect you;

-Stop complaining about your situation, just make changes;

-Stop making excuses as if you are helpless and go forth with determination;

-Stop focusing on negative behavior and begin to seek opportunities that are new for you and your advancement;-Stop discouraging your friends if (he or she) tries to do better (envy);

-Stop telling your children, he or she will not be anything of value

Stop giving your child names that will automatically telegraph who he is, if you can. We need the "field" to be fair from the start!

-Stop treating your child as a friend; instead use parental love to teach character and values; and use discipline when needed.

It Is Not Too Late to Start:

-**Start** respecting each other, including yourself and partner,

-**Start** being a good listener, be willing to compromise when conflicts arises and develop ways to resolve disagreements,

-**Start** encouraging your child to avoid gang-type relationships and being influenced by negative school peer-groups,

-**Start** being a motivator, team-builder and a mentor for your child,

-**Start** encouraging youth black pride in their appearance,

-**Start** encouraging positive attitudes within their communities,

-**Start** encouraging them toward joining the military or reserves, early.

-**Start** encouraging good self-confidence with enthusiasm,

-**Start** accepting past mistakes and move pass them with humility.

-Start teaching your child Alternative Dispute Resolution concepts (ADR) in an effort to encourage them to deal better with conflicts,

-**Start** encouraging your child to be respectful of others and more grateful when they see positive behaviors and empathy, and

-**Start** encouraging them to be more responsible as our Father would want them to and seek religious teachings from others you know.

Chapter 26

EPILOGUE

I t is with sincere thinking that today's environment easily tells each of us that one's belief in equal employment opportunity has taken on a new mindset. We are watching Fox New (The Five), occasionally. It appears that they are so angry and negative that opinions are steering viewers to be negative towards anyone that is reasonable, social-minded, and shows empathy for others.

The civil rights Revolution has been caught up in the crisis of victory; a crisis which may involve great opportunity or great danger to its fulfillment.

~ A. Phillip Randolph, 1965

The experience I received from working for the government, private business, social non-profits organizations, and my family and friends have positioned me well. As I was instructed by my family long ago, pray that others see me as a good person the same as I will certainly see them; Enough is Enough!

"Because as I look back over my life and think about the many more instances where I was involved in trying to make a difference in others' lives through my unique mediate skills, I realized that each situation was sent to me through His grace. That is why I am so grateful to have had the opportunity to solve many human and civil rights disputes in the workplace. I can truly say I have been blessed! Yes, I have done my best and I have a testimony."

I often was told I smiled a lot, and God has allowed me to be a good listener!

Finally, it seems that learning about diversity in this very confusing world has created a known disregard for respecting differences. Throughout my many years training folks toward accepting one another, I must have missed something.

Is it because people generally think of bad things when it has to do with people of color? In the past, this country was called the "melting pot" meaning that we were supposed to blend together like a soup or something. Well, those before us were trying to use "empathy as a tool to gather us to do this." Today, I, personally realize that Trump, prior to his presidency, gave his followers a bottle of poison to disrupt 33society aimed to minimize the influence and impact of hateful ideology and far-right extremism. As one that mediated human rights concerns, I and others like me tried to encourage respect and a peaceful workplace.

I am very discouraged along with others that "hate" has surfaced throughout our country. Did it begin with, President Obama. Was it because of "diversity?"

As the years have passed, I and many others, that are dedicated toward human rights for all, need to continue to try to hopefully address these "fooled individuals." We feel that their children will not fall for this racial-crazy-like behavior once they become a more caring adult. Therefore, you can succeed if humility is a part of their everyday life, everywhere. This is what I believe.

About The Author

President Joe Biden's Lifetime Achievement Award

History Maker & Washington, DC Hall of Fame Inductee

Pierpont Morgan Mobley, MLS, MA, CM

Pierpont Morgan Mobley's passion for civil and human rights, politics and government was impacted by his experiencing discrimination while growing up in Washington, D.C. His lifetime work as a Civil and Human Rights advocate and activist expands over 40 years of which 16 of those years were spent at the White House serving the Johnson, Ford, Nixon and Carter Administrations.

His detail from the National Security Agency to the White House Administrative Offices, where his commitment and performance was noticed led to his promotion and appointment as the first African American to work in the White House Personnel Office. While he had many successes in this role, he is most proud of the fact that he wrote the first Affirmative Action Program for the White House and 11 Executives Offices of the President during the Carter Administration. He recruited and coordinated many Black hires for White House Office and was often mediating many employee and management disputes.

Upon leaving the White House, he went on to work in other federal agencies under the Carter, Reagan, Bush and Clinton Administrations in leadership positions championing civil and human rights in the areas of equal employment, gender equality and LGBT rights. As Chief of EEO for (SCS), USDA, he was selected to serve on task force in 1993 that wrote the first Sexual Orientation Policy for the White House and played a major role in the Black Farmers Class Action suit against USDA. He resolved many EEO cases.

During all these years, Pierpont also served his country by spending twenty-one years in the D.C. Army National Guards as a Miliary Police Officer and an Affirmative Action Coordinator and HR in race relations Senior Sergeant.

Pierpont's commitment to his field of work also extended to his Washington, D.C. community in several key areas. He voluntarily mediated many of family disputes at the Superior Court, and was appointed by Mayor Anthony Williams as a Commissioner to the D.C. Office of Human Rights/Rehabilitation Council and served on the Luke C. Moore Academy High School Board for over 20 years under the Late Dr. Reginal Elliott and the late Honorable Luke C. Moore for whom the school was later named and the former Chief Judge of the Superior Court, the Honorable Eugene Hamilton. I had an 85 percent resolution rate at these informal stages. I often received commendations from many individuals for my ability to seek amenable resolutions between disputing parties.

His tenure on the board resulted in him mentoring many students seeking a second chance at education and raising monies for the Board's scholarship fund. Also appointed HR Commissioner and served as Communication Coordinator for OAG. He is a current member of Delegate Eleanor Holmes Norton Military Service Academy Nominations

Committee. He taught Conflict Resolution concepts at Howard University.

Upon retiring, he founded The JPM Group, LLC a Human Resources and Management training and consulting firm providing expertise in all his work-related areas to the public and private sector clients. Pierpont is still actively engaged with his community by volunteering with nonprofit organizations dedicated to empowering males to positively embrace fatherhood and thrive in their families and mentoring at risk male high school students on manhood and character building. His longstanding involvement in working on various Democratic projects, at both the local and national levels, has garnered him an honorable reputation among community leaders and politicians in the DMV.

Pierpont's life work has been recognized by the History Makers in 2013, D.C. City Council Ceremonial Resolution for his longstanding community outreach, civil and political involvement in 2020, and Induction into the Washington D.C. Hall of Fame in 2020. He has been a faithful member of the Second New St Paul Baptist Church in Washington, D.C. who over the years has recognized his faithful service.

In summary, he has trained many employees and management officials in a variety of disciplines all related to social change and individual and team development. His training in conflict resolution was for the primary purpose of building self-confidence toward navigating in the workplace more effectively.

Mobley attended Antioch School of Law, where he received his MLS/MA degree in equal employment opportunity/employment law. He completed BA studies at Federal City College and PA, Upper Iowa, University.

During the past 30 years or so, I have been a mentor and have volunteered in our community to serve on the following boards and initiatives:

-Served on the Office of Administrative Appeals Committee for two years

-Serves on the Washington Gas (Ward 5) Committee (EAB: Education Advisory Board) for four years.

-Serves on the Armstrong Tech Alumni (HS) Committee (Chair) for 5 years.

-Served on the DC State Rehabilitation Council, for 3 years.

-Serves on the SASB (Military Selective Service Board) for seven years under DC Delegate Eleanor Norton's Congressional Standing Committee.

From a political point of view, my wife and Pierpont played major roles in at least five (5) local democratic campaigns in the District of Columbia. In fact, the word was out long ago that we were *The Power Couple from Ward 5.*

1. Wilkerson, Isabel (Apr 2021). How Did the Great Migration Change the Course of Human History. National Public Radio. Ted Talks.

2. Ibid

3. National Park Service. Bolling vs Sharpe. https://www.nps.gov/places/washington-dc-john-philip-sousa-junior-high-school.htm

4. Ibid

5. Findlaw. Bolling vs Sharpe. https://caselaw.findlaw.com/us-supreme-court/347/497.html

6. The legal problem in the District of Columbia is somewhat [347 U.S. 497, 499] different, however. The Fifth Amendment, which is applicable in the District of Columbia, does not contain an equal protection clause as does the Fourteenth Amendment which applies only to the states. But the concepts of equal protection and due process, both stemming from our American ideal of fairness, are not mutually exclusive. The "equal protection of the laws" is a more explicit safeguard of prohibited unfairness than "due process of law," and, therefore, we do not imply that the two are always interchangeable phrases. But, as this Court has recognized, discrimination may be so unjustifiable as to be violative of due process.

7. At the beginning of the twentieth century, Armstrong Manual Training School and M Street High School were the only two high schools in DC that admitted black students. Armstrong was built between 1900 and 1902 and was originally called Manual Training School and was the African American counterpart to Manual Training School #1, which was intended for white students. In 1903, Manual Training School became Armstrong Manual Training School in honor of General Samuel Chapel Armstrong, a white commander of an African American Civil War regiment and founder of the Hampton Institute, attended by Booker T. Washington. The original Armstrong Manual Training School had carpentry, machine, foundry, blacksmith, and lathe workshops. Laboratories were provided for chemistry, physics, and photographic work. The building also contained seven classrooms, a study hall, and drafting room.

8. In 1960, Blacks made up the majority of the city's population, outnumbering whites by nearly 10 percent. Although DC did have a large middle-class Black population, the income differential between whites and Blacks widened in the 1950's and 60's. In 1960 the Census reflects a white median annual income of $7,692 while that of Blacks was $4,800.

9. Merida, "Before Chocolate City", 18.

10. The 1968 Washington Riots in History and Memory.

11. The Chesapeake and Potomac Telephone Co., usually known as C&P Telephone, is a former d/b/a name for four Bell Operating Companies providing services to Washington, DC, Maryland, West Virginia, and Virginia.

12. The school pioneered a comprehensive law clinic education model espoused by Edmond Cahn, a law professor at Columbia University and Edgar's father in the 1930s. His concept was to train lawyers like doctors in a clinical model, as opposed to the pure Langdell Case method use by Harvard and most other law schools, and to use those lawyers in training to provide legal services to those unable to afford lawyers. The original school was located on 16th Street, NW and its law library a block away on Crescent Place, NW in Adams-Morgan near Meridian Hill Park. The school now operates as the University of the District of Columbia David A Clark School of Law.

13. Igbo, N. (Feb, 2019) Black History Month: What is it with Us and Cadillacs? nikigbo.com

14. Uppity was a derogatory term liberally used in the Jim Crow south. Uppity was often used as a term in reference to Black people who they felt were above oneself, self-important, jumped up, haughty, pert, putting on airs. The thought was that Black people should not seek to climb the social ladder.

15. With Kennedy's unexpected death, the need for a clear way to determine presidential succession, especially with the new reality of the Cold War and its frightening technologies, forced Congress into action. The new President, Lyndon Johnson, had known health issues, and the next two people in line for the presidency were 71-year-old John McCormack (the Speaker of the House) and Senate Pro Tempore Carl Hayden, who was 86 years old. Section 1 of the 25th Amendment made it clear that the Vice President became President when the presidency became vacant under three circumstances: death, resignation, and removal from office. Section 2 gave the President the power to name a new Vice President, if that office became vacant, with the permission of Congress.

16. National Archives, Civil Rights Act of 1964

17. 15. Naftali, T. (2019) Ronald Reagan's Long-Hidden Racist Conversation with Richard Nixon. The Atlantic

18. FOIA is the Freedom of Information Act which gives a person the right to request access to Federal records. There are two distinct types of records: archival and operational.

19. Civil Rights Record of Gerald Ford, 1949-1976" the Ron Nessen Papers, Gerald R. Ford Presidential Library.

20. Alcorn, C. (2023). Jimmy Carter's Pivotal Role in Georgia's Black Civil Rights Struggle, Interview with Meredith Evans, Historian. Capital B. Atlanta.

21. The Civil Service Reform Act of 1978 is intended to provide Federal managers with the flexibility to improve Government operations and productivity while, at the same time, protect employees from unfair or unwarranted practices. As part of civil service reform, a reorganization of the agencies administering the Federal personnel system was proposed and approved. The Civil Service Commission (CSC) was abolished, and the Office of Personnel Management (OPM) and the Merit Systems Protection Board and its Special Counsel were established in its place; the Federal Labor Relations Authority was established in place of the Federal Labor Relations Council; and the Equal Employment Opportunity Commission was given responsibility for enforcing equal employment laws in the Federal agencies. Government Accountability Office (GAO).

22. For most of the 20th century, the United States Bureau of Mines (USBM) was the primary US government agency conducting scientific research and disseminating information on the extraction, processing, use, and conservation of mineral resources. The Bureau was abolished in 1996.

23. Strawbridge-Robinson, K.. (June 29, 2023). Clarence Thomas Wins Long Game Against Affirmative Action. Bloomberg Law.

24. Totenberg, N. (July 9, 2023). Supreme Court Dissents and rejoinders with respect and disrespect. National Public Radio (NPR) https://www.npr.org/2023/07/09/118 274177/supreme-court-dis sents-and-rejoinders-with-respect-and-disrespect

25. Ibid.

26. Anderson, J. (June 29, 2023). Clarence Thomas Benefited from Race-Based Preferences Throughout His Career. Slate. https://slate.com/news-and-politics/2023/06/affirmative-action-ov er-clarence-thomas-vote.html

27. Black farmers once owned 14% of all farms in the country—today (2022) they own just over 1%, in part due to governmental discrimination.

28. Ref: Obama Signs Measure Funding Black Farmers settlement, CNN Wire, Dec, 2010

29. L. Crawford (March, 2022) 5th Circuit Grants Intervention to Black Farmers to Defend Critical USDA Debt Relief Program, Lawyer's Committee for Civil Rights Under Law

30. US Court of Appeals 5th Circuit, Case: 21-11271 Document: 00516249617

Got an idea for a book? Contact Curry Brothers Publishing, LLC. We are not satisfied until your publishing dreams come true. We specialize in all genres of books, especially religion, leadership, family history, poetry, and children's literature. There is an African Proverb that confirms, *"When an elder dies, a library closes."* Be careful who tells your family history. Ensure their values are your family's values? Our staff will navigate you through the entire publishing process and we take pride in going the extra mile in meeting your publishing goals. Improving the world one book at a time!

Curry Brothers Publishing, LLC
PO Box 247 Haymarket, VA 20168
Office: (888) 726-1824

Visit us at www.currybrotherspulishing.com

www.ingramcontent.com/pod-product-compliance
Lightning Source LLC
Chambersburg PA
CBHW051159120626
46547CB00012B/1127